Great Ways to Integrate
in the Classroom

21st Century Curriculum: Activities That Will Keep Your Students Engaged

Chris Clementi
Kidsnetsoft.com

Great Ways to Integrate Technology in the Classroom

21st Century Curriculum: A Necessity to Thrive in an Uncertain World

ISBN 978-0-7414-6185-8

Printed in the United States of America

Published November 2010

INFINITY PUBLISHING
1094 New DeHaven Street, Suite 100
West Conshohocken, PA 19428-2713
Toll-free (877) BUY BOOK
Local Phone (610) 941-9999
Fax (610) 941-9959
Info@buybooksontheweb.com
www.buybooksontheweb.com

Acknowledgments

This book was written by me, with the help of students, family, friends and members of online communities who create applications that make integrating technology fun, easy and exciting. My partner, Paul Schurtz, has been very supportive throughout this process. My daughter, Marianne, has been a great sport allowing me to work on this book when I should have been tending to her needs. No worries, she wasn't totally abandoned. I also would like to thank my cousin Debby for providing me beautiful photos and support. I thoroughly appreciate feedback from my family, friends and students. My students have taught me a great deal. They give me ideas that I couldn't get from a book. They help me grow as an educator and I truly appreciate them. I am genuinely thankful for the Open Source Community, Web 2.0 resources and other creative sites that have made this book possible. Some of those wonderful resources include Animoto, Audacity, GIMP, Glogster, Google, NVU, Paint.NET, Photostory, Switch Zoo and Voicethread. I am grateful for Microsoft's software, which has resulted in some of the greatest projects in my classroom. I would also like to thank the following people for giving me permission to use their images: Darell Vanaman; Marianne; Ilovepandas.org; Debby Lee; Richard Muller; Robert L. Pitman; and Switch Zoo. I also couldn't have created some of my examples without the images I obtained at the Colorado Renaissance Festival.

Table of Contents

Table of Contents

Table of Contents

Feedback

First of all, I would like to thank you for purchasing my book. I have spent over a year compiling resources and ideas to make your life as a teacher easier. I know how hard it can be to teach. This book is meant to make your life easier and more pleasant in the classroom. There are many handouts available in Word 2003 so that you can customize the lessons according to your content and interests. The technology will change after you purchase this book, however, the ideas will be there for years to come. I will be more than happy to provide feedback to you or your students. Some of the lessons are based on material on my website, which will only get better. My goal is to make your life easier with classroom ideas. My CD is packed with user friendly handouts and video to help your students master tools and concepts about technology integration. I will do my best to accommodate your classroom needs in relation to lessons in this book. Your feedback will help me as a classroom teacher and publisher. If you visit the Download link of my website, you can access copyright friendly images for a variety of projects. Most images were provided by myself, friends and family. Most of my images are from Colorado because that is where I reside. As I make my way around the country and hopefully overseas, more images will be added to that site.

My classroom website: http://www.kidsnetsoft.com
My e-mail: kidsnetsoft@gmail.com

About the author and how to use this book: This book is designed to make classroom assignments more interesting and fun. As a teacher and webmaster, I know how important it is to engage students in a meaningful way.

About the author: I have been a middle school computer application's teacher for over six years. I have created my entire curriculum. I continue to refine lessons so that they are meaningful and interesting for my students. I believe that if our students are engaged, they are learning. My website has been online for over six years and I plan on having it available as a resource for teachers as long as I am breathing. My website is intended to accompany this book. If you have any questions about the content of the website or book, please feel free to contact me at kidsnetsoft@gmail.com. In addition to creating hundreds of lessons, I am a staff developer, presenter and life long learner.

Changing technology and resources: With the constant changing of online resources and technology, this book needs to have a versatile dimension. Because some of the wonderful resources found in this book might not be available by the time you choose to use this book, my online site will provide current information and alternatives if necessary. You can also contact me at kidsnetsoft@gmail.com

Copyright: Copyright is an issue we all must face in the classroom. I don't claim to be a copyright expert, but I am constantly trying to keep abreast on this topic. There is a section on the CD that capitalizes on copyright. This user friendly handout discusses sites that can be used for educational purposes. It is in the PDF folder titled copyright. There are several online resources that are user friendly to educators and students as long as there is no intention to publish the work. Some sites that are in the Public Domain allow publication with some restrictions as long as it is for educational purposes. Students are always encouraged to read a website's term of use before publishing online. If some of the resources are outdated, search for copyright friendly images and read the terms of use just to be on the safe side. I will continue to add images on my website for classroom use. http://www.kidsnetsoft.com/html/download.html

Prerequisite: Some of the activities require the completion of other lessons. Sections will notify you if a prerequisite is necessary.

Design: Design will be consistently reinforced in lessons because in addition to content, design is a critical attribute to being able to communicate in our visual world. If students are to create a product that provides an audience with content, they also need to be aware that fewer people will want to read their information if they don't pay attention to aesthetics.

Saving Work: It is a great habit to always encourage students to find a safe and reliable location to save their work. I have all my students create a main folder for my class. Within my class folder, I have them create several folders to stay organized. For example, all word documents are saved in a Word folder, while all images are saved in an images folder. They are constantly reminded to rename any large, quality images they get off the Internet. Too often, students click save and don't pay attention to where and how they save their material. This is a very bad habit. If you are on the same page as them, it will be easier to find their work if they have trouble finding their digital resources. Besides, this is a life long learning habit that needs to be established.

CD: The CD has several handouts that are designed to be picked up and worked on by students via the computer to eliminate printouts. Students should save the handouts in a safe and organized location. Their work can be graded on the computer. All documents are created in Microsoft Word 2003 or 2007. Students can access these documents using the school's network. Have them copy the document and then paste it in their own organized folders. Most school districts have a network that students should be able to access with a login. If this isn't an option, I have provided portable document formats (PDFs) that are ready for printout. If you can't read a PDF, you can download Adobe Reader for free: http://get.adobe.com/reader/. In addition to having several handouts, the CD has video to further assist in your learning experience. Each activity will tell you where you can pick up lessons, handouts and videos.

Mac Shortcuts: Most of the lessons provide shortcuts for a PC. To get Mac shortcuts, check out this fabulous website: http://lixlpixel.org/mac-keyboard-shortucts/

NETS: If you go to the ISTE site and click on NETS (National Educational Technology Standards), you can get the most current standards for students, teachers and administrators. http://www.iste.org/

Prerequisite to Using this book: This section gives great tips prior to diving into the activities.

Image searches: When getting images from Google or other search engines, it is good to have a basic foundation about safety, quality and searching techniques. The following examples are from using Google as a search engine.

Keep it safe: You can keep relatively safe if you make sure the safe image search is on while getting images for projects. You can determine if the safe search is on under the search section of the image search. If it says Strict SafeSearch is on, surf away. If is shows that SafeSearch is Off, use the following steps to solve the problem.

1. If it shows the Strict SafeSearch, is Off, click on the arrow for options. Scroll down and select **Strict**. This will reduce the possibility of finding inappropriate images.

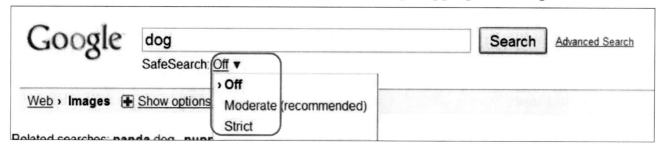

2. The page will reload with more appropriate images after selecting Strict.
3. This isn't bullet proof, but it will minimize exposure to inappropriate images.
4. Students should never click on a questionable image to reduce seeing inappropriate material.
5. Students need to be cautious of what words they use to search for images.
6. Students can also click on the **Advanced Search** option to specify what kind of images to search.

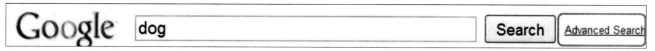

7. The Advanced Search will give other meaningful and helpful searching options such as image size, type and shape.

If you aren't safe, you might get bit!

By making the student aware of safety precautions, they become more empowered and responsible for making good choices.

Maintain image quality: In the majority of cases, students should always get larger images. If you want to guarantee larger images and quality, take note of the following steps.

1. To get larger images, you should be able to access the different image sizes when doing an image search.
2. Select the desired size under the **Any size** option that might pop up on the left hand part of your window. Google's search façade may change by the time you read this page.
3. When you find an image you want to use in a project, double click on the small icon to get the larger image or click on the **See full size image** link to get the larger image.

 See full size image
855 x 1013 - 388k - jpg - www.my-photoshop.com/.../02.jpg
Image may be subject to copyright.
Below is the image at: www.my-photoshop.com/bydesign/Print_Design-Bo...

4. If the larger image isn't available, have your students keep looking. Quality shouldn't be sacrificed.
5. I can't think of any case where I would stretch an image for a project. If it has to be stretched, get another image.
6. If you visit the **Advanced** Search link for images in Google, you can also specify what size, type and shaped images you want in your search. Depending on what you are looking for, this could narrow your image search to the point where you have limited options. If this is the case, find the large image you want and crop it if necessary.
7. If you find an image that is great, but it has parts of it that need to be cropped, you can use several tools of image editing programs to crop out unwanted material or content. If you Google "online image editors" you will find some great sites to crop your images.

Before Cropping!

After Cropping!

Effective and Efficient Searches: Researching online can be very overwhelming. The following tips should make searching for information more efficient if done properly.

1. When conducting a web search, encourage students to carefully and wisely choose appropriate words. For example, if they want to find information on baby chickens, they should type in baby + chickens in the search category. If they type in chicks, they are more likely going to get a variety of very inappropriate website options.
2. It would be a good idea to visit the **Advanced Search** link when using Google.

3. Once you click on the **Advanced Search** page, you can type in the various categories.

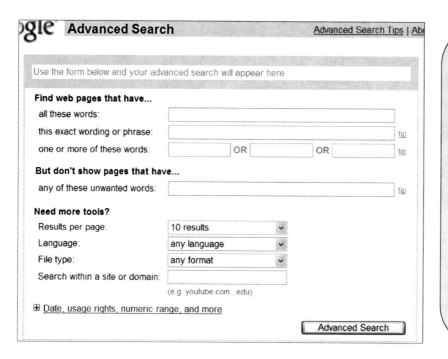

Cool Stuff:
This search allows you to refine your searches. You can even add words that you don't want in your search. Change the language if you wish. In the **Search within a site or domain section,** you can specify only education sites by typing .edu or government by typing .gov

4. If you want details on how to search more efficiently, you can click on the **Advanced Search Tips** link.

Searching Wisely: It is important to give students effective searching techniques so they can find valid information efficiently. Researching online can be very frustrating. Without the necessary tools and know how, students are less likely to find what they need in a timely fashion, which can and will lead to frustration.

5. Students are encouraged to consider viewing U.S. government documents to increase their chances of getting valid information. To quickly get government sites on the topic at hand, they can type in .gov in the **Search within a site or domain** of an advanced search window.

6. One could add the following criteria to an advanced search window or type in the following for a decent search on the poor health conditions of child workers in the United States during the 1800s: **"child labor" + "united states" + "poor health" + 1800s + site:.gov**

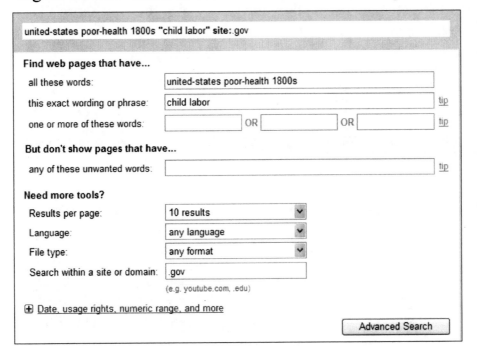

Government Sites: U.S. Government sites are considered to be some of the best resources to use for research. To get government sites, you can type **site:.gov** in your keyword search. If you wanted education sites, you would type **site:.edu**.

7. When searching for certain topics that tend to be associated with other topics, you can run into problems. For example, if searching for information on foxes, the mammal, you might get unnecessary and unwanted images. To maximize your chances of getting information or images on the animal, you could type in **foxes +animals** (no space after the plus sign) This also holds true with the minus sign. To eliminate certain searches, type in the minus sign and then the keyword to avoid unwanted search results. For example, if you were looking for jaguar, the animal, you would type in **jaguar –car** in your search. If you still get cars in your search, you could try **jaguar –car +animal.** Students might need to be creative in the choice of words they use for a search.

8. In this book, there are lessons that discuss how to determine if a site is valid or not. Talk to your librarian about credible sites. S/he may have some great resources, which can reduce the stress of finding credible information. It is a great skill, however, for students to determine if sites are reliable.

Activity 1: Manage files and folders. This activity is essential for being organized on the computer. Believe it or not, many students aren't in the habit of creating folders and staying organized. This will be a great activity before starting any lessons. The handout, **fileManagement** can be picked up in the **PDF folder**

Directions: The following activities might help prepare you for future activities and assisting you in maintaining good file management. This assignment gets you familiar with locating and saving from the applications you might use for projects or work. Directions are helpful for Microsoft Office 2003 and 2007.

1. Double click on **My Computer** on the desktop or go to your start menu to locate **Computer**.

2. Double click on the **Drive** or location on your computer that you need to save your projects. Usually, when using your home computer, you either save on your Desktop or C: drive. Your teacher will let you know where to save your folders and documents.

3. Select **File | New | Folder** or right click in a blank area of the location you are creating a new folder and choose **New | Folder** from the drop down menu.

Share with	▶	
New	▶	📁 Folder
Properties		

4. Type **myProjects** and press on the **Enter** Key.

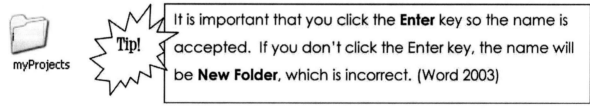

myProjects

Tip! It is important that you click the **Enter** key so the name is accepted. If you don't click the Enter key, the name will be **New Folder**, which is incorrect. (Word 2003)

5. Once you have named the folder, open it by double clicking.

6. Recreate the following folders inside of **myProjects**:

☐ **excel**

☐ **images**

☐ **PowerPoint**

☐ **sound**

☐ **word**

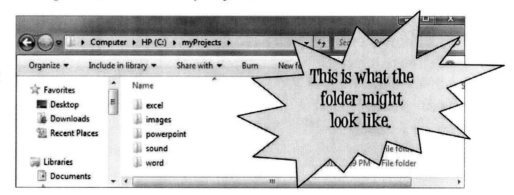

This is what the folder might look like.

Activity 2: Create your own book summary based on the cover of the book. Students will have fun making their own hypothesis about the book based on the book cover's presentation.

Tip: The following illustration is an example of what the document looks like if you were to print the PDF. To save paper, you can get each handout to your students on computers and have them type up their answers. Going paperless is the way to go if you have access to computers. I am able to grade most of my students' work at their computers, giving them direct feedback. It sure saves on grading papers at home and wasting resources.

1. Students can fill out the worksheet titled **summarizing books** in the **PDF folder** of the CD or pick up the word document via a computer transfer. The document that can be completed on the computer is found in the **word folder** titled **summarizing books**. See tip below or read the CD section of page 2.

Summarizing Book Covers

Directions: Look at a variety of book covers from the library or by going online. After looking at a variety of book covers that you have never read, fill in the table below.

#	Book Title	Author	Brief description of cover's illustration	Your brief summary of what you think the book will be about.	Actual book summary from a credible online source or from the actual book.
1	PDF Example				

2. Look at several book covers and titles. You can gather books from the library or go online to search for book covers and titles.
3. Students will write down the book title, author's name, brief description of the book cover's illustration, and a summary of what they think the book will be about.
4. Finally, they read the actual book summary and write it up in the final column.
5. Let students know they must pick books they have never read and are unfamiliar with.
6. You might choose to preselect books you are almost sure they have never read.
7. Some teachers might want to get their students excited about reading certain books for the year by having them complete this activity.

1. Students will do this lesson as a prerequisite for creating their own clipart for future projects. This lesson can be considered valuable because it allows students to customize clipart to compliment any color scheme they choose for a project.
2. Students love this project because it allows them to be creative while they manipulate clipart and learn about different tools.
3. I always encourage students to experiment with as many tools in Microsoft Word as possible because there is no right or wrong way to do this assignment.

Example: The following is an example of the handout titled **clipart2003** in the **PDF folder**. This document provides user friendly, step by step directions to transform Microsoft clipart. Another user friendly handout is also available for 2007, titled **clipart2007**.

Manipulating clipart images in **Microsoft Word 2003**

Directions: Follow these steps to insert different colors and patterns of certain clipart images.

1. Open **Microsoft Word** by going to the **Start** menu. Choose **All Programs | Microsoft Office | Microsoft Office Word**
2. Select **Insert | Picture | Clip Art** from the main menu
3. A menu should pop up on the right hand side of your window. Type in the name of the clipart you are searching for. To guarantee clipart images only, select **Clip Art** under the **Selected media file types.** Click on the image you want and it will automatically load on your document (keep in mind that this activity doesn't work on all the images)

4. Click on the **Text Wrapping** tool
5. Select **Behind Text**

If the text wrapping tool isn't showing, double click on the image. When the Format Picture window pops up, click on the Layout tab. Then you can choose Behind Text

Activity 4: Draw your own clipart. Students can learn how to make their own clipart. This activity is a prerequisite to Activity 5.

1. Students can have access to handouts and video to help them learn how to make their own clipart.
2. Once students complete this practice lesson, they can transform their knowledge to create their own masterpieces. This will free them from having to worry about copyright laws because they will be able to use their own creations.

Example: The following is an example of one of the handouts that demonstrates all the various tools needed to complete this assignment. It is in the **PDF folder** and it is called **making clipart**. Another document accompanies this lesson so students can practice tracing clipart with the most appropriate tools. This document is found in the **word folder** titled **tracing clipart**. Students need to pick this document up digitally. The video is in the video folder titled **tracing clipart**.

1. Open Microsoft Word by choosing **Start | All Programs | Microsoft Office | Microsoft Office Word** or double click on its icon if it's on your desktop.
2. Save your document by choosing **File | Save As** from the main menu.
3. Navigate to your **word** folder and name the document **clipart creations**.
4. You might use the following tools to create **your** clipart: To access the tools, locate your **AutoShape** tools. If it isn't showing, choose **Tools | Customize** from the main menu and select **Drawing** from the **Toolbar's** option.

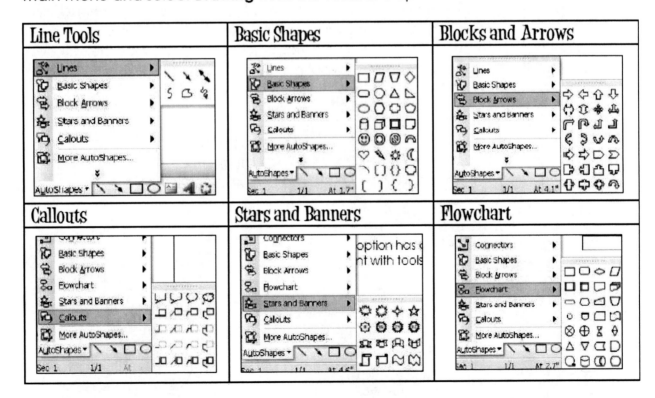

Activity 5: Title and decorate a book cover. Activity 3 and 4 should be completed so students can adequately design book covers with clipart if necessary.

Students will read several book summaries. You can preselect a variety of books you might be interested in having students read. Once you have preselected the books, cover the book cover with your own customized instructions, or use the cover template titled **book covers** in the **PDF folder.** If students skim through the book, they might see the title. If so, encourage them to come up with their own title. If students aren't publishing their work, they can use images online or copyright friendly images that allow publishing for educational purposes.

Handout: This print-out can be found in the **PDF folder** titled **book covers.** It can be temporarily pasted on a book cover and handed to students to complete. Encourage students to pick a unique and readable font for the title. See page 12 for examples of how students can visually illustrate a book. All images used are either created by me in Word 2003 or taken digitally to avoid copyright violations.

Activity 4 on page 10 will teach students how to create their own clipart. It is a very popular and fun activity for students.

Give Me a Title and Illustrate Me

Directions:

1. Read the book summary
2. Come up with a different title
3. Illustrate the cover page using the computer.
4. Computer tools can include drawing tools in Microsoft Word, Paint, Photoshop, etc.
5. Quality images from the Internet can also be used as a background.

I was made with drawing tools in Microsoft Word.

Think about it: By drawing your own images, you can publish your work. Otherwise, copyright laws will most likely be violated.

Examples of book covers based on the book summary of several books. The actual title and author of each book is posted above the example.

500 Places to Take Your Kids Before They Grow Up, by Holly Hughes

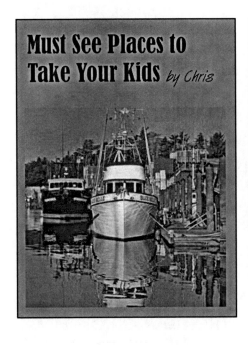

1001 Facts About Sharks by Joyce Pope

Guide to Colorado Historic Places, by Thomas Noel

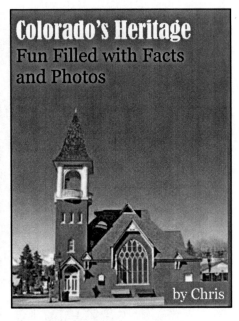

Girls in Pants, The Third Summer of the Sisterhood by Ann Brashares

Secrets in the Hills, an American Girl Series by Kathleen Ernst

Foul Facts History, the Awful Truth by Amber Grayson, Jamie Stokes

Activity 6: Create a poster on endangered animals. This lesson can be tweaked for a variety of topics. It includes handouts and examples. Student will learn great tools and techniques about design. This knowledge can be transferred to other projects. Check out the example titled **endangered poster example** in the **poster_unit folder.** (See following page)

1. Students will complete a document called **plan_endangered** in the **poster_unit folder.** The following is an example of what the document might look like. You can find the example in the **poster_unit folder** titled **plan_endangered_example.** The **plan_endangered** document in the **poster_unit folder** can be customized for your classroom interests. For example, you can reword the categories and directions for whatever topic you want covered for the poster unit.

2. Students are asked to just write the facts without putting complete sentences. This tends to prevent plagiarism.

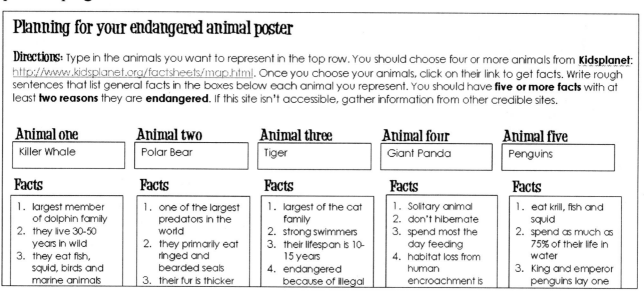

Planning for your endangered animal poster

Directions: Type in the animals you want to represent in the top row. You should choose four or more animals from **Kidsplanet:** http://www.kidsplanet.org/factsheets/map.html. Once you choose your animals, click on their link to get facts. Write rough sentences that list general facts in the boxes below each animal you represent. You should have **five or more facts** with at least **two reasons** they are **endangered.** If this site isn't accessible, gather information from other credible sites.

Animal one	Animal two	Animal three	Animal four	Animal five
Killer Whale	Polar Bear	Tiger	Giant Panda	Penguins

Facts	Facts	Facts	Facts	Facts
1. largest member of dolphin family 2. they live 30-50 years in wild 3. they eat fish, squid, birds and marine animals	1. one of the largest predators in the world 2. they primarily eat ringed and bearded seals 3. their fur is thicker	1. largest of the cat family 2. strong swimmers 3. their lifespan is 10-15 years 4. endangered because of illegal	1. Solitary animal 2. don't hibernate 3. spend most the day feeding 4. habitat loss from human encroachment is	1. eat krill, fish and squid 2. spend as much as 75% of their life in water 3. King and emperor penguins lay one

3. Once they have completed the document, they can start their poster by following the directions in the **endangered handout** in the **poster_unit folder**

6. When the **WordArt Gallery** appears, choose a **style** and then click **OK.**

These are examples of some of the different styles. The shadow and 3D styles were removed. There will be more on shadow and 3D later.

Examples of the Endangered Animal Poster: This poster is designed to be informative and attractive. Consistency is a major part of design. There is font consistency and an efficient use of space.

Killer Whales: Killer whales are the largest member of the dolphin family. They can live 30 to 50 years in the wild. They eat fish, birds, squid and marine animals. They are endangered because of pollution and chemicals. The pollution leads to diseases and reproduction problems. *Photo courtesy of Robert L. Pitman*

We love momma!

Polar Bears: Polar bears are one of the largest predators in the world. Their diet primarily consists of ringed and bearded seals. Their fur is thicker than any other bear. They are endangered because loss of sea ice which affects their hunting. They are also threatened because of illegal poaching. *Photo Free clipart now*

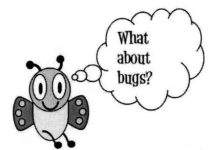

What about bugs?

Rhinos: White rhinos live on Africa's grassy plains. They reproduce roughly every two and a half to five years. Their single calf will not live on its own until they are about three years old. They are endangered primarily because of habitat loss and poaching. Unfortunately, they are being killed for their horns for medicinal purposes in some Asian countries. *Photo by Richard A. Muller*

Penguins: Penguins eat krill, fish and squid. They spend approximately 75% of their life in water. The males keep their offspring warm for roughly 65 days while the females search for food. They are endangered because their habitat is changing. Other reasons for endangerment include oil spills, pesticides, construction and competition with humans. Illegal egg harvesting is also leading to further threats for the penguins. *Photo National Science Foundation*

Giant Pandas: Giant pandas are solitary animals. They don't hibernate. They spend most of their day eating. They are endangered because of habitat loss from humans competing with them for resources. They are also illegally poached. *Photo iLovepandas.com*

Activity 7: This lesson is designed to help students improve their writing skills. They use the built in thesaurus to transform simple words. For example, the word bad is in the story 10 times.

1. Students need to pick up the story **Worst Day** in the **word folder** to edit.
2. Before students start to edit this elementary level story, they need to make sure certain settings have been set up.
3. They need to choose **Tools | Options | Spelling and Grammar** from the main menu in Word 2003. (2007 directions in **PDF folder** titled **readability statistics for word 2007**)
4. They need to make sure the **Show readability statistics** is checked off at the bottom of this window. If these steps are unclear, pick up the sh**ow readability** in the **PDF folder.**

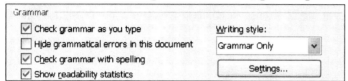

5. After making sure the **Show readability statistics** option is checked off, they can choose **Tools | Spelling and Grammar** or **F7**from the main menu. They may have to fix necessary spelling and grammar errors. Otherwise, a window should pop up stating the reading level of the story.
6. They can record their reading level at the bottom of the story where it states **started at**: The reading level is indicated by the **Flesch-Kincaid Grade Level**. If it says .9, that means it is not even first grade. I question such grade levels, but if students make improvements to their story by adding more complicated sentences and if they change smaller words to larger words, their reading level will increase and the story should be more interesting.
7. How to change a word: **a)** Select the word **b)** Choose **Tools | Language | Thesaurus** from the main menu or click on the **Shift + F7** keys. Options will pop up. Once you find a word that you want to use instead, click on the drop down arrow next to the word and choose **Insert.**

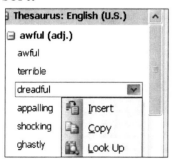

Have students expand their vocabulary by clicking on other words. For example, if you click on dreadful, several synonyms of dreadful will pop up. This is a great way for students to learn more words and enrich their story.

8. Students are told they can't use words they aren't able to pronounce and if they don't know what it means. They are also discouraged from having too many adjectives to describe a noun. One of my students had roughly ten adjectives to describe one word.
9. Make up your own rules for this activity. Student really like to see their progress as they embellish their stories. You can do this with your own stories.

Example One: Reading level .9 (This is only paragraph one)

The Worst Day EVER

I had a bad day when I woke up today. I fell out of bed and hit my head on the nightstand. I had a bad time finding my clothes. I couldn't find my pants, shirt and shoes. I had to wear dirty clothes. Other bad things continued to happen as I got ready for school. My glasses were broken when I found them. I fell down the stairs when I was going to the kitchen to eat breakfast. At breakfast, I had a bad time. I spilled cereal on myself. I also dropped my banana on the floor.

Example Two: Reading level: 4.0

The Worst Day EVER

I had an appalling day when I woke up this gloomy, depressing and miserable morning. I fell out of my inflexible bed and hit my head on my maple nightstand that was purchased from my wealthy and pretentious relatives who reside in New Haven Connecticut. Though the nightstand is beautiful and exotic, I despise them. Well that is neither here nor there. Let's get back to my wretched morning. I had a difficult time finding my school clothes. I couldn't find my recently purchased denim jeans that I was looking forward to wearing for various reasons. My soft cotton shirt with an embroidered penguin was no where to be found. Lastly, the shoes that everyone envied were found under my bed destroyed by my sister's misbehaving and unruly puppy. I had to go to the laundry room and choose from the dirty clothes pile. You can only imagine the wrench. My parents can't bother to keep us in clean clothes. I know, you are probably thinking, why can't I do laundry. I have enough to do in the house if you don't mind. Other horrible things continued to happen as I got ready for school. My glasses were broken into tiny bits and pieces when I found them. Apparently, they somehow ended up under our couch. My father, who is always unaware of his surroundings, managed to sit on the couch and crush my glasses in the process. Because I am near blind without my glasses, I fell down our winding and narrow stairs as I rushed to the kitchen for what I thought would be a delicious and warm breakfast. At breakfast, my day continued to become more unbearable. I spilled soggy and stale cereal all over my already disgusting pants. I also dropped my mouth-watering and totally favorite fruit, the banana of course, on our tile kitchen floor that hasn't been cleaned since the Dark Ages. Could my day get any worse than this, I asked myself, as I decided to forfeit breakfast because I feared I would do unimaginable things to my stomach? With very little time left before school starts, I realized it was time to head on out of my possessed home.

Activity 8: Do your students have trouble following directions? This activity will most likely trick most of your students. When students realize they should have read the directions a little more closely, they say, "You got me!"

Following Directions: Have students pick up the document titled **computerTerms** in the **word folder**. You can always customize the worksheet to compliment your content. Check to make sure the link for this project is available. You may have to use another website.

About this assignment: Problem 18 states: Don't answer questions 1-17. The remainder of the problems will require a response. It is humorous to watch students look up all the terms while working problems 1-17, especially since they are told the assignment needs to be completed by the end of the period.

Computer terms: http://www.webopedia.com/

Directions: Following directions is a very important strategy to be a better learner. Sometimes people make serious mistakes if they don't follow directions. This assignment should be easy and fun for anyone that follows the directions. Don't plagiarize. Read problems 1-22 before answering the following questions. The teacher will not help in this assignment, so you are on your own. If the web address above can't answer the questions, use an appropriate key word search using Google.

Question pertaining to computers	Answer
1. What does html stand for in reference to website development?	
2. What does the term phishing mean?	
3. What does the abbreviation URL stand for?	
4. What is an IP address?	
5. What is a hard drive?	
6. What is software?	
7. What is a floppy disc?	
8. What is a wav?	
9. What is a gif?	
10. What does the abbreviation gif stand for?	
11. What is a monitor?	
12. What are function keys?	
13. What does the abbreviation PC stand for?	
14. What is an operating system?	
15. What is real time?	

Activity 9: This lesson is great for getting students to practice their creative writing. Students use a website called Switch Zoo to create a creature that they write a story about. This activity has been used to make a one page website in my classroom. Audio stories have been created around this creature. See Activity 10.

Example: The following is an example of the handout titled **switchZoo** found in the **PDF folder**. This document provides user friendly, step by step directions on how to create creatures on this site. Once they have created their animal, they can write a story about their creature, discussing its habitat, diet, enemies and more. An example of the final story is given on the handout. See below:

Creating stories about unique creatures: This lesson involves the creation of a unique animal using Switch Zoo. If this isn't an option, you can create your own images using Photoshop or other image editing programs.

1. Go to the Switch Zoo website: http://www.switchzoo.com/zoo.htm
2. Select one of the animals from the oval shape or select the Rhino that says Switch Zoo **Animal List**.

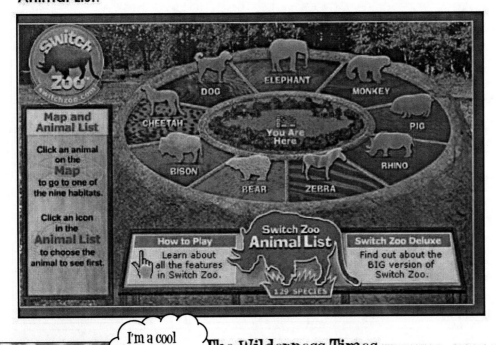

The Wilderness Times Thursday, July 6, 2006

I'm a cool example!

Breaking News in the Northwestern Montana by Chris Clementi

The Johnson's, a family of five, were enjoying their summer vacation until they were confronted by a mysterious creature in Montana's Grangewood National Forest. In the early morning, The Johnson family decided to go foraging for berries when they heard strange sounds approximately one mile from their camp. They were terrified from this sound because it was a noise they were totally unfamiliar with. The younger daughter, who usually

Activity 10: Create audio stories about your creature. The audio stories can be put on websites. The only concern is your district may block such sites. Audacity ® is an audio editing program that can be downloaded for free. If it isn't available, have your tech person set you up. Audio editing programs tend to motivate just about any student. Make sure you are equipped with headphones and microphones. Some of the sites or lessons we will be looking at later in the book have recording capabilities. It really does add to ones curriculum.

Following Directions: You can print out the handout **radio** found in the **PDF folder. (see example of page one on the following page)** This can be re-used over and over to save paper of course. Students need to pick up the document titled **audioStories** in the **Word folder.** You can watch the video titled **audacity** in the **video folder.**

1. Make sure you have an audio editing program. You can download Audacity at http://audacity.sourceforge.net/
2. You may need someone with administrative privileges to download the program and make sure everything is working accordingly. It is so worth investigating.
3. Once you have experimented with Audacity and it has recording capabilities, you can start the lesson.
4. It is highly recommended to write the stories in advance. Students can pick up **audioStories** in the **word folder**. The following is an example of the document.

Audacity Writing Brief Stories for Recording in Audacity

Directions: You will create two or more brief stories that contain 100 words or more to be recorded for your one page website. Read the example for ideas. Once you have an idea, **type in the rows** under the **Written Story** category. The following example is set up to add 10 seconds of songs from your favorite bands. You would have the last 10 seconds of the song and then have your story. The end of your final recording would then have the first 10 seconds of another band.

Example of a story: Thank you, that was ACDC, now we bring you breaking news from Jane Johnson. On January 7th, 2007, a strange creature was sighted on the side of the road near Bristol. People interviewed were unable to get a close look at this creature, but insisted it looked like a bear and a bison. Others swore it looked like a bear with a monkey's tail. Whatever this creature is, townsfolk are talking about how we should call in the National Guard. Some people are buying weapons and getting more locks for their homes. The police department is trying to alleviate their fears by increasing security in the region. In the meantime, the FBI has sent agents to investigate the sighting. If the creature is caught, they want to conduct studies on this animal. If you have any leads to the location of this creature, call 1-800-888-news. Thanks for that story Jane and now we bring you Aerosmith.

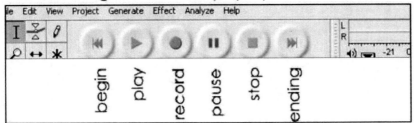Audacity Radio Effects in Audacity

1. Create a folder somewhere safe on your computer and name it Audacity to be organized.
2. Open Audacity by double clicking on the Audacity icon or choosing **Start | All Programs | Audacity**
3. The following window will pop up. Please take note of each function.

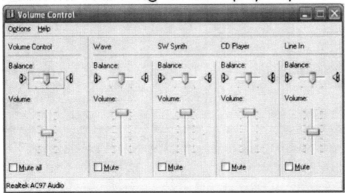

4. Before recording, check the settings to make sure you have recording capabilities by **double clicking** on the **volume control** found in the lower right section of the task bar.
5. If that icon isn't available, choose **Start | All Programs | Accessories | Entertainment | Volume Control**
6. When the following window pops up, make sure nothing is muted.

Volume Control	Wave	SW Synth	CD Player	Line In
Balance:	Balance:	Balance:	Balance:	Balance:
Volume:	Volume:	Volume:	Volume:	Volume:
☐ Mute all	☐ Mute	☐ Mute	☐ Mute	☐ Mute

Options   Help

Realtek AC97 Audio

7. You might want to **Level** out all the **volume controls** so they are roughly in the middle. **Experiment!**
8. You might want to **minimize** the **volume control** so you can access it later if necessary.
9. To record your voice, make sure that **Microphone** is selected.

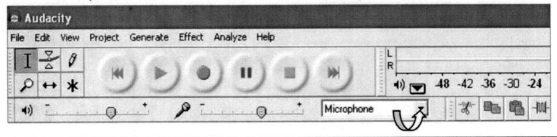

Examples of literacy and audio combined: Students create a one page website about a creature they generate using Switch Zoo. They create hyperlinks to sites about the creature's diet, enemy, facts and more. The sites are usually random and unique, to encourage creativity. One of the most interesting aspects of this assignment is creating audio stories. When a user clicks on Story One, they get to listen to a story, with radio effects, about the website's creature. Listen to the actual story by visiting http://www.kidsnetsoft.com/chris_c/index.html

The Gem MoBear

This unique creature is the result of the unification of a Bison, Kodiak Brown Bear, a Wooly Spider Monkey and a Gemsbok. They live in the lush forest of Bolounge. Because of their unique make up, the animal has interesting characteristics. It gets some of its sight qualities from the Wooly Spider Monkey. For instance, it can perceive many details in shades of green that humans are incapable of seeing. Like the Kodiak Brown Bear, the cubs weigh approximately 85-100 grams at birth. They also have a hump of fat on their shoulders. They get their speed from the Bison, which gives them the capability of running 30 miles per hour. They are also very strong swimmers. They hibernate in the winter and don't come out until spring. Like the Wooly Spider Monkey, they live together in troops of 5-25. Unfortunately they didn't get all their traits from the Wooly Spider Monkey. They are a very violent animal that will intimidate almost any animal. The only animal that

Links

- Diet
- Enemy
- Facts
- Habitat
- News

Audio

- Story One
- Interview
- Story Three

Writing brief stories for the audio part of projects

Directions: You will create two or more brief stories that contain 100 words or more to be recorded for your one page website. Read the example for ideas. Once you have an idea, **type in the rows** under the **Written Story** category. Stories should be written at grade level or higher. Use the readability statistics option in Microsoft Word to continually check your grade level.

Story #	Written Story
Story One	Thank you, that was ACDC and now we bring you an interview with Kevin and Jane that will make your mind spin. **Kevin**: Hello Jane, glad you can talk to us about this recent sighting of a mysterious creature. **Jane**: No problem Kevin, it is great to inform the population about circumstances that could be dangerous to their safety. **Kevin**: What can you tell us about this animal that was seen running down Main street on the evening of January 1st? **Jane**: I was preparing to interview some former gang members when I saw a creature that looked like the combination of a bison and Kodiak bear running at great speeds through traffic. **Kevin**: Was it chasing something? **Jane**: I wasn't able to tell because of the chaos that took place from fear and panic. **Kevin**: Was anyone injured? **Jane**: Two people were hospitalized when the creature tumbled over them while they were crossing the street. **Kevin**: Will they be ok? **Jane**: Fortunately, they have minor injuries and have already been released from the hospital. **Kevin**: Does anyone have the whereabouts of this creature? **Jane**: Unfortunately, the animal hasn't been spotted since the Main street incident. **Kevin**: Can you give the public any safety measures? **Jane**: Just be cautious and be more aware of your environment. **Kevin**: Is there anything else you would like to add to this interview? **Jane**: If you see this animal, call 1-800-be-cautious Kevin: Thank you Jane, and now we bring you Pink Floyd.
Story Two	

Activity 11: Read the title of several current event articles. Choose five or more and rewrite the articles in your own words. Re-title the articles and accompany them with an image. You might want to look at Activity 6, the poster unit, so you have more ideas about design. They can also create their own newsletter with this information.

Example: The following is an example of the word document titled **Current Events** in the **word folder**. This document needs to be picked up by students to edit. Online links for current events: http://www.kidsnetsoft.com/html/current.html

Current Events:

Directions: Read the titles of 10 or more Current Events from any of the following sites: http://www.kidsnetsoft.com/html/current.html List the titles in the first table below. Choose at least five of the articles to read based on your interest level of the title. Use the second table to rewrite the articles and titles. Rewrite the stories in your own words. With your rewritten stories and titles, you can visually represent them in a poster or a newsletter. Don't forget to add images.

Write down 10 or more current events titles in the following table:

#	Title of Current Event	#	Title of Current Event
#1		#2	
#3		#4	
#5		#6	
#7		#8	
#9		#10	
#11		#12	

Write down 5 or more of the titles that interested you the most. Briefly summarize each article so that you can re-write the story in your own words later. Re-title each article.

Story #	Titles	Write Title Information	Rewrite Story
One	Original Title		
	Your Title		
Two	Original Title		
	Your Title		
Three	Original Title		
	Your Title		
Four	Original Title		
	Your Title		

Activity 12: Student will either write their own poem or find a poem that they want to present in a multimedia presentation. They will break down the poem into small parts to be visually represented. Everything that needs to be picked up will be in the **photostory** folder. The first thing that needs to be completed is their **plan poem** document. You can see an example of what that plan might look like when completed by picking up the **plan poem example.** See pages 25-26.

Example: The following is an example of the tutorial **photostory handout** in the **photostory folder.** This handout gives step by step examples of how to create a Photo Story presentation. Don't forget to pick up the rubric. You can customize it to your classroom needs. If you Youtube kidsnetsoft, you can see some poetry examples.

Creating presentations with Photo Story 3 by Microsoft
This program can be downloaded for free. Google Photo Story and click on the Microsoft link to download this application if necessary.

1. Before starting this project, you need to have your images prepared and saved in a folder. To maintain quality throughout your presentation, the images should be the same size. If resizing images isn't an option, make sure you get images that are roughly 640 X 480 pixels. If you use small images and stretch them, you will lose quality.
2. You should complete the **plan poem** document, which requires you to break down several parts of a poem and get images.
3. To open the program if it isn't on your desktop, choose **Start | All Programs | Photo Story 3**
4. When the following window pops up, select one of the following options and then click on the **Next button.**
5. In this case, **Begin a new story** was selected. If you had a project already created and it needed editing, you would choose **Edit a project**

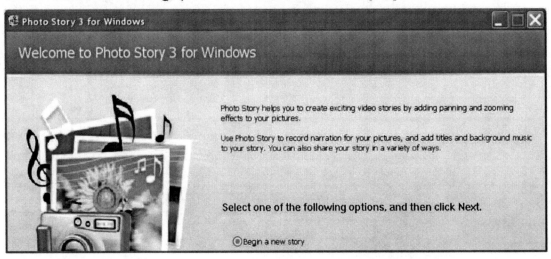

Example: The following is an example of the word document titled **plan poem** in the **photostory folder.** This document needs to be picked up by students to edit. You can find online links for poetry by visiting my classroom site http://www.kidsnetsoft.com/html/poetry.html. You might want to double check that the poetry links are appropriate and suitable for your class. You might want to check to see if the sites are appropriate for your classroom expectations.

Directions: find a poem that you would like to visually represent in a Photo Story presentation, PowerPoint or movie. In this case, Photo Story will be used as the application. The poem should be broken into segments of a few lines per image. The segment should end naturally. The images should be saved as image1, image2, etc. This will help with organization. You should have at least 10 images to represent 10 different segments of a poem. Be sure to give the website name as your image source in the **Image Source** column. To add another row to the table, click in the last column of the last row and hit the tab key of your keyboard.

Name of Poem: Replace this text with the name of your poem
Author of Poem: Replace this text with the name of the poem's author

#	Segment of a poem	Image saved	Image Source
1		image1	
2		image2	
3		image3	
4		image4	
5		image5	
6		image6	
7		image7	
8		image8	
9		image9	
10		image10	
11		image11	
12		image12	
13		image13	
14		image14	
15		image15	
16		image16	
17		image17	

Directions: find a poem that you would like to visually represent in a Photo Story presentation, PowerPoint or movie. In this case, Photo Story will be used as the application. The poem should be broken into segments of a few lines per image. The segment should end naturally. The images should be saved as image1, image2, etc. This will help with organization. You should have at least 10 images to represent 10 different segments of a poem. Be sure to give the website name as your image source in the **Image Source** column. To add another row to the table, click in the last column of the last row and hit the tab key of your keyboard.

Name of Poem: Irena Sendler, a woman to know
Author of Poem: Chris Clementi

#	Segment of a poem	Image saved	Image Source
1	Irena Sandler, a woman to know.	image1	musicalwren
2	Many horrors she did spare,	image2	memorial-church
3	So that children could grow.	image3	communitynorthbc
4	During great danger spite her foe,	image4	mistermarks.com
5	What she did others wouldn't dare.	image5	strategypage.com
6	Irena Sandler, a woman to know.	image6	dickiebo
7	An ambulance driver on the go,	image7	Wikimedia
8	And a barking dog guards couldn't bear.	image8	Flickr
9	So that children could grow.	image9	kentlawncare.com
10	The terror of millions made it an all time low,	image10	Life
11	As conscious humans realized how unfair.	image11	Flickr
12	Irena Sandler, a woman to know.	image12	esteblognoesparati
13	Children smuggled to-and-fro,	image13	Wikimedia
14	With demons unaware	image14	Flickr
15	So that children could grow.	image15	Wikimedia
16	Her heroism risked a major blow,	image16	
17	as Nazis considered such acts with flair,	image17	
18	Irena Sandler, a woman to know,	image18	irenasendler

Activity 13: Students are going to complete an Internet Hoax Unit. This unit is designed to help students determine if information online is a hoax or not. This is a critical skill that students should master if they are to be literate in today's world. If they can search effectively and efficiently online, they will be better informed citizens, especially if they rely on the Internet for their information.

Example: The following is a screenshot of the online unit. You can go to: http:www.kidsnetsoft.com/webquest/html/index.html to access the web quest. The process link is packed with activities that can be downloaded and completed by your students. The handouts for this unit can be picked up in the **hoaxes folder.**

The Johnson's, a family of five, were enjoying their summer vacation until they were confronted by a mysterious creature in Montana's Grand wood National Forest. In the early morning John son family decided to go foraging for berries when they he.. They approximately one mile for their camp. They were terrified from th sound because it was a noise they were totally unfamiliar with. The younge daughter, who usually had no fear, let out a blood curdling scream that sent shivers

Hoax or Not?
by Chris Clementi

Welcome to "Is it a hoax or not? "

FOLLOW THESE STEPS

1. INTRODUCTION

2. THE TASK

3. THE PROCESS

4. RESOURCES

5. EVALUATIONS

"I'm not upset that you lied to me, I'm upset that from now on I can't believe you""

Friedrich Nietzsche
1844-1900

Last updated August 1, 2006. Copyright © 2006 Chris Clementi

Great resources: Some of these resources are real and some are fake. They are worth investigating. http://www.kidsnetsoft.com/html/bogus.html

Website Rubric: This rubric can be used to help determine if sites are credible or not. The higher the score, the greater chance it is credible. However, the Factuality criteria score can pretty much weed out good sites from bad sites. You can pick up the **website rubric** in the **hoaxes folder.**

Criteria	3	2	1	Rating
Author Identification.	The author's name is easy to find and it appears as though s/he would be an authority on the subject.	The author's name can be found, but s/he may or may not be an authority on the subject.	The author is unknown.	
Sponsoring organization.	A well-known respectable organization is clearly identified as a sponsor of the site.	A sponsoring organization can be identified, but its reputation in relation to the topic is questionable.	No sponsoring organization can be identified.	
Last updated	Current Event: updated within the last month. Historical Topic: updated within the last year.	Current Event: updated one to six months ago. Historical Topic: updated one to two years ago.	No date is shown or information is outdated: Current Event: more than six months old. Historical Topic: more than two years old.	
Author contact	The author's contact is easy to find and is available through a direct link.	The author's contact information may be difficult to find/is not available through a direct link.	No author contact can be found.	
Factuality	The website gives just the facts and seems to be free from opinions or bias.	The website appears to be factual, but the author's opinions are frequently revealed.	Facts are questionable, based mostly on the author's opinions.	
Source of information and ethics	The author explains where most information came from and provides direct links to original information.	The author occasionally explains where information came from but does not provide direct links to original information.	The author never explains or identifies the source of information.	

Hoax_or_not?: Determine if the images and information are real or fake!

Example: This is an example of the document that will assist students in determining if e-mail messages or websites are giving fake information. I got the idea to do this lesson after I started getting several e-mails that seemed questionable. Whenever I get an e-mail that states be sure to send this to so many recipients, I become skeptical. That is usually a red flag that it is most likely a scam. I research online, using an efficient key word search and then I e-mail the sender of the scam the website address of a credible source to let them know they just sent me fake information. Hopefully this will break the chain so to speak. Some great sites that help determine if information is a scam or not is http://snopes.com/; http://urbanlegends.about.com/; http://www.breakthechain.org/; http://www.museumofhoaxes.com/. Be sure to check these sites out. Unfortunately, they may have ads that aren't appropriate or images that are disturbing. You can add your own images and information on this document to meet the needs of your classroom. (Students will often use U.S. government sites to assist in this project.)

Pick up the **hoax or not** document in the **hoaxes folder**. You can also download these from the hoax or not website at Kidsnetsoft.

Directions: Read each possible e-mail hoaxes and research the topic at hand. Determine if it is a hoax or not. Wr explanation in the description column of this worksheet. Make sure you copy and paste the keyword search that to solve the following problems. Cite two web sources that confirm your answer.

#	Is this a Hoax?		Keyword Search	Web addresses that confirm your answer
1		This photo was taken of this tourist on top of the World Trade Center moments before it was hit on September 11, 2001		URL:
				URL:
2		Roger, the owner of this 87-pound cat believes its size is attributed to her thyroid.		URL:
				URL:
3		An Israeli woman accidentally swallowed a fork after inserting it down her throat in order to remove a cockroach.		URL:
				URL:

29

Gathering "Facts" using the Find Function. You can pick up **find function** from the **hoaxes folder.** Using the find function is a handy tool if you are trying to locate information as quickly as possible. You have to use efficient key words or the assignment can become tedious and boring. This is a great skill that student should have. The only draw back, however, is if they are on a fake website using the find function. This will prevent them from reading the site, which might cause them to actually question the material. One assignment required 6th and 7th graders to find "facts" from a site on the tree octopus. By the end of the lesson, the majority of my students were ready to save an animal that doesn't exist. The site on South America was created to add more depth and trickery. It is not as easy for students to determine it is a fake site unless of course they are world travelers and experts on South America. Check out the **find function answers** to see the truth!

Directions: To get to the following website, hold down the Ctrl key and click on the following link: South American News Use an efficient keyword search to find your answer. To get to the **Find Function**, click on the **Ctrl + F** keys of your keyboard on the website and type in the keyword to find the information more quickly. The first one has been done as an example.

#	Question	Keyword used	Answer
1	Looking at the home page, who donates most of the images for this site?	donate	Students and professors from various Colleges and Universities in South America donate images to this site.
2	Looking at the home page of this site, who is Vicente Yanez Pinzon?		
3	What was significant about the year 1516 in Argentina?		
4	Why has the language been influenced by the Germans and Scandinavians in Argentina?		
5	What is causing Bolivia to be one of the wealthier nations in South America?		

Distinguish Fact from Fiction. You can pick up **research site** from the **hoaxes folder.** Students should complete the **find function** activity prior to completing this document. You can get the answer key, titled **research site answers** in the **hoaxes folder.** Teachers can change the answers as they may change with time. The answer key is a guide. Not all students will have the same conclusions because only a few of the lies and truths are being evaluated. There are many possibilities per country. As the author of the website, I plan to add more information. For the record, the only truth about the images on each page, except the update page, is the photographer's name. You might want to divide the problems among your students because this assignment is extensive.

Have your students e-mail me if they find flaws in my site or answers. kidsnetsoft@gail.com...I will be happy to edit and send revisions.

For further assistance, check out my truth page: http://www.kidsnetsoft.com/southAmerica/truth.html

Webpage: Home page		
#	**Facts:**	**Resources:**
1	Sao Paolo University is the largest state university in Brazil.	Britannica.com
2	Considering the site mentioned Pics4Learning, I looked up squirrel monkeys and found the actual image. It did state that Terry Rosengart is the photographer of the photo	Pics4Learning.com
3	When looking at the terms of Pics4Learning it stated that they have 1000s of images donated by teachers, students and amateur photographers.	Pics4Learning.com
#	**Fiction:**	**Resources:**
1	The only information I could locate on Vicente Yanez Pinzon was that he commanded the *Niña* in 1492–93 and remained with Columbus throughout the expedition.	Britannica.com

More on the Find Function. You can pick up **find function2** from the **hoaxes folder.** This assignment has been done several times with my 8th grade students. Even though the 8th graders either did this activity on the Tree Octopus in 6th or 7th grade, they forgot my intentions of tricking them. They are too busy determining which key word search to use so they can answer the questions as quickly as possible. They don't even bother to look at the website address: http://www.idiotica.com/encyclopedia.Two students questioned the website address. I discretely asked them to play along as the others diligently researched the false website.

Research Efficiently

Directions: This lesson is to demonstrate how to find information more quickly when researching online. Click on the hyperlink for each set of problems. To get to the website, hold down the **Ctrl** key and then click on the link. Determine a keyword for each problem and use the find function online. For example, in problem 1 you will click on the **Ctrl + F** keys to get the find function and type in expectancy. If a certain keyword doesn't help you locate your information, try another keyword search. Spelling is critical for this to work.

X Find: expectancy	Previous Next	Options ▾	1 match

#	Question	Answer
Use this site to answer the following questions: Beluga Whales		
1	What is the life expectancy of the Beluga whale?	
2	What is the status of the Beluga whale?	
3	What is the average length of the Beluga whale?	
4	What is the average weight of a Beluga whale?	
Use this site to answer the following questions: Mars		
5	Who was the 1989 Nobel Prize for Science?	
6	What is the length of day on Mars?	
Use the hyperlinked sites to answer the following questions:		
7	How many square miles of tundra covers the Earth's surface?	
8	How many square miles do deserts occupy on earth?	
9	Which cactus is able to extract moisture from even very arid desert air?	
10	How many square miles of rainforest are lost every day?	
Use this site to answer the following questions: Albert Einstein		
11	When was the *Theory of Relativity* published?	
12	What was the month, date and year of Albert Einstein's death?	

Comparing information from Idiotica Encyclopedia and Credible websites

On Beluga Whales:

Idiotica's Claims	National Geographic	U.S. Department of Congress
Life Expectancy of a Beluga Whale is: 75 to 100 years	**Life Expectancy of a Beluga Whale is:** 35 to 50 years	**Life Expectancy of a Beluga Whale is:** 35-50 years
Status: Not Threatened	**Status:** Threatened National Geographic	
Food: Carnivorous; eats mostly tuna and harp seal, known, in rare cases, to attack humans.	**Food:** fish, crustaceans, and worms	**Food:** "Beluga whales are diverse eaters, with more than 100 prey species identified including salmon, capelin, herring, shrimp, Arctic cod, flounder, and even crab."
Average Weight: 7 tons	**Average Weight:** 1 to 1.5 tons	
Average Length: 32 Feet	**Average Length:** 13 to 20 ft	
"Male Belugas tend to be solitary, while females raise their young and socialize in large groups called "fronds."	"Belugas generally live together in small groups known as pods."	

On Mars

Idiotica's Claims	Google Search	Nasa
Who was the 1989 Nobel Prize for Science: Melvin Schperling	Couldn't locate such a person	

33

Gathering Information from Websites. You can pick up **gathering information** from the **hoaxes folder.** You may need to change the website and example to a site that you wish your students to evaluate. As mentioned earlier in the rubric for website evaluations, one should avoid relying on "facts" from websites that have too many opinion statements. If the students look at the website name, they may ask questions. That is where we want our students to be.

Directions: visit as many links as possible on the following website: http://www.idiotica.com/encyclopedia/ Fill in the conditions below to learn why this site is not a valid resource. A few sections were filled in as an example. You should fill in at least 20 additional boxes below to assist you in your final evaluation. At least 5 boxes should be filled under the Fiction category. All opinion words should be made as red text. Copy and paste all URLs that were used to discredit this false website. See table below for pasting URLs. Type in the actual fact in the table below that disputes the fiction of this website. Two categories were filled in while reading about Beluga whales on the website. Notice that when it was read that the life expectancy of the Beluga whale was 75-100 years, National Geographic's site stated otherwise. National Geographic, being a credible site, was used to dispute the information on Idiotica encyclopedia. If Idiotica encyclopedia isn't available, find another site to evaluate.

Opinion Words	Facts	Fiction
"The Southern Army fell under the supervision of General Ulysses S. Grant, a maniac and drunkard."		The Life Expectancy of the Beluga whale is 75 to 100 years.

Fact	URL
Average lifespan in the wild: 35 to 50 years	http://animals.nationalgeographic.com/animals/mammals/beluga-whale.html

34

Activity 14: Students need to be aware of potential online threats so that they can protect themselves and their computer. The following lessons will help make students more aware of problems such as phishing attempts, virus threats and more. Phishing is a widespread problem where perpetrators attempt to gather personal information so they can basically steal your identity. Once your identity is stolen, they can and will threaten your livelihood. You should never give any personal information to e-mail solicitations.

Pick up the **problem or not** document in the **scams folder**. This is a template and it can be customized for your classroom. See the example of how these problems could be answered on the next couple of pages.

Problem or Not?

Directions: Read each problem. Research the problem to answer the question. Give the site that confirms your answer. Give a brief description to justify your answer. Paste the entire web address that helped you answer each question in the last row where it says Website:

Problem One	Question	Answer in Detail
McAfee Inc., a web security company estimates that nearly three-quarters of all sites dealing with Internet searches for popular phrases like "free screen savers" or "digital music" attempt to install some form of advertising software in visitors' computers. Once lodged there, spyware can reduce a PC's processing power, slow its functioning, and even cause it to crash.	With this information, will you avoid downloading free screen savers or digital music?	
Website:		

Problem Two	Question	Answer in Detail
The FBI is sending information to recipients to educate them about their ties with Facebook. By clicking on the link, you can view the article. The subject line might read FBI vs. Facebook.	Would you click on the link to read the article? Why or why not?	
Website:		

Directions: Read each problem. Research the problem to answer the question. Give the site that confirms your answer. Give a brief description to justify your answer. Paste the entire web address that helped you answer each question in the last row where it says Website:

Problem One	Question	Answer in Detail
McAfee Inc., a web security company estimates that nearly three-quarters of all sites dealing with Internet searches for popular phrases like "free screen savers" or "digital music" attempt to install some form of advertising software in visitors' computers. Once lodged there, spyware can reduce a PC's processing power, slow its functioning, and even cause it to crash.	With this information, will you avoid downloading free screen savers or digital music?	I would definitely not download "free screen savers" or music, especially if I am being solicited online. If I want music of screen savers, I will go to reputable sites to get them. I would prefer that my computer operate more efficiently. Downloading from the Internet needs to be done cautiously. It is also a good thing to get anti spyware software.

Website: http://www.msnbc.msn.com/id/13757388/

Problem Two	Question	Answer in Detail
The FBI is sending information to recipients to educate them about their ties with Facebook. By clicking on the link, you can view the article. The subject line might read FBI vs. Facebook.	Would you click on the link to read the article? Why or why not?	I would not click on the link. If I wanted to find out information about the FBI and Facebook, I would Google it and find a credible site to let me know if there is a dispute between the two identities. According to Snopes, a reputable site that informs the public about hoaxes states that by clicking on this link, you will download a virus. This virus will allow the perpetrators to take over to facilitate other crimes.

Website: http://www.snopes.com/computer/virus/fbi-facebook.asp

Problem Three	Question	Answer in Detail
You receive an e-mail with "230 dead as storm batters Europe" in the subject line. Along with that subject is a video attachment or link to a website.	Would you open the video? Why or why not?	I would not open up the video attachment or click on a link. You should never open links or attachments from people you don't know. This is another attempt to get the user to download a virus. Unfortunately, antivirus software has a difficult time detecting it to fix it.

Website: http://www.snopes.com/computer/virus/storm.asp

The fake site: I got an e-mail from someone phishing. Their e-mail mentioned that my account may have been tampered with. I clicked on the link and entered a fake login and e-mail address. I was brought to this screen that looks just like PayPal's website. If I would have submitted information, I could have lost some serious security. Take note of the website address of the person phishing and then take note of the actual PayPal website address. Quite different, wouldn't you say?

Actual URL: http://2755705615:20/webscr/index.php?www.paypal.com/cgi-bin/webscr?cmd=_login-run=update.user.8djjjgu7d87ds7f67dsf6tdsf6t4rwkjge8r7f932hh4378hgwfg8rfgort8we7gf we7gft7we6gf34grt793tgw6grt97873gf73762346rf327rgg9f6g37fg23g6f23riholgbklerk36t nfierAf?

The real site: Actual legitimate URL of PayPal: http://www.paypal.com/ Notice the navigation of the real PayPal and the fake site above. This is very easy to do.

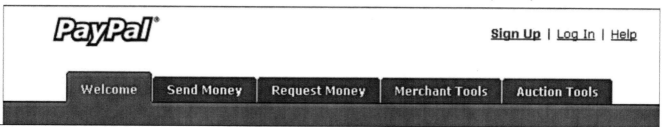

Activity 15: Fun with Searches: Once you know how to search effectively and wisely, you can fully appreciate using it for so many wonderful activities. The next series of lessons will require Internet access. All the activities for this section will be in the **Internet folder.** There will be templates for various classroom projects.

Scavenger Hunt This lesson can be easily customized for a variety of curriculums. If necessary, you can delete or add columns to add or remove themes. This template is called **scavenger hunt template.**

Directions: Use appropriate key word searches to find the correct answer for every question below. Type in the keyword search that helped you find the answer. You must only use credible websites. The first one is an example.

Question	Keyword Search	Website Host	Answer
What bug is capable of firing a hot, toxic fluid to deter predators?	bug + firing a hot toxic fluid + predators	Science Daily	African bombardier beetle

Picture Mystery: This activity allows students to be online detectives and figure out information on images with clues. They have to experiment with key word searches to locate their information. The following page gives an example of what the teacher would pass out to the student. As the teacher, you can customize the template for projects you are working on in class. For instance, if you are a history teacher, you could show artifacts or historical places. When setting up the clue, don't give too little or too much information. The students need to problem solve. Locate this document, titled **Picture Mystery Template**, in the **Internet folder.**

Directions: Solve each problem by filling out the table below. The key is to use efficient key word searches. You may have to continuously rephrase or reword your searches so that you can find your information more effectively. Add the keyword search when it is the one that gets you the good result. You can do an image or web search to find your answers. Be sure to cite the credible website that you used to get your answers.

Picture	Clue/Question?	Keyword Search	Answer
You can also watch the auto-shape tips video in the video folder to learn how to add images to AutoShapes.			
Website Address:			
Website Address:			

1. Before editing the template, resave it as something other then template. You want to keep the template intact. Name it according to the project. For instance, the example being shown on the following page could be titled places.
2. To add an image, select the rectangular **AutoShape** in the Picture cell and choose the drop down arrow of the paint bucket. Choose **Fill Effects (Windows 2003)** or **Picture (Windows 2007)**. When the Fill Effects window pops up (**2003**), choose the **Picture** tab. When you locate and select your image, choose **Open** or the **Select Picture** option.
3. Once completed, place your document in a location that students can pick it up.
4. Be sure to keep your original backed up in case it gets accidently edited or deleted by a student.

Example of the Picture Mystery assignment. This document can be found in the **Internet folder.** It is titled **Picture Mystery**. The answer key is **Picture Mystery Answers.**

Directions: Solve each problem by filling out the table below. The key is to use efficient key word searches. You may have to continuously rephrase or reword your searches so that you can find your information more effectively. Add the keyword search when it is the one that gets you the good result. You can do an image or web search to find your answers. Be sure to cite the credible website that you used to get your answers.

Picture	Clue/Question?	Keyword Search	Answer
	Beulah red marble is what gives this State Capitol a distinctive look. It took six years to install this marble, from 1894-1900. Where is this capitol?		
Website Address:			
	What is the name of this church in Mesilla, New Mexico?		
Website Address:			
	How many miles of art work does the Pueblo Levee Mural Project have along the Arkansas river?		
Website Address:			
	Name this famous hotel that might possibly be best known for its role in "The Shining", a Stephen King novel.		
Website Address:			

Activity 16: Fun with Images: This section will give students opportunities to have fun with projects that involve images and design. A video is available in the **video folder** called **autoshape tips.** It will give tips on how to add images to the quilt. This video will be helpful for other activities in this book.

Making a Quilt: This activity requires students to design a quilt based on your desired theme. The following is an example for Colorado. It could be on a country of study, inventions of the 20th century, a visual book report, endangered animals, problems of the 21st century, etc. The template can be picked up in the **Design** folder titled **quilt template.** Each box has a square AutoShape that requires the student to add an image using the paint bucket tool. You can view the **autoshape tips** video available in the **video folder.** This is an example of what a quilt can look like. You can access this as a **PDF** in the **Design** folder titled **quilt example.**

Quilt Details The quilt has a total of thirty squares to be filled with images shaped like squares. The video **autoshape tips** will give great tips on design.

Menu Design This activity requires students to design a menu for a hypothetical restaurant. The template they need to pick up for this lesson is called **menu template**. This lesson is in the **design folder**. A PDF, titled **menu example** is also available. Students can make any necessary changes on this template to compliment the theme of their restaurant. The **autoshape tips** video is available in the **video folder**. It will give design tips on filling in autoshapes. All the blank auto shapes can be replaced with customized images.

Welcome to Regina's Favorites: Regina's restaurant is one of Denver's favorites. It has a cozy atmosphere that is inviting to anyone. The aromas are captivating while the flavors are savoring. It has been voted Denver's Best in Fine Dining.

Address:
555 Regina Road
Denver, CO 80220

Hours of Operation
Sunday-Thursday 3:00-10:00 p.m.
Friday-Saturday 3:00-11:00 p.m.

T-Shirt Designers: This activity requires students to design T-Shirts. In this example, it is for environmental causes. You can change the wording of the directions to fit your classroom needs. Pick up the document in the **design** folder titled **t-shirts**. You can pick up the video, titled **t-shirts**, in the **video folder**. The video is for Word 2003. The **autoshape tips** and the **tracing clipart** videos will help students who have Word 2007.

Directions: You have just been hired to design T-shirts for an environmental organization. They want the T-shirts to motivate audiences to be responsible and do the right thing when it comes to protecting the environment and its inhabitants. Come up with a saying and a design for each T-shirt. To learn how to design your T-Shirts, watch the t-shirt video.

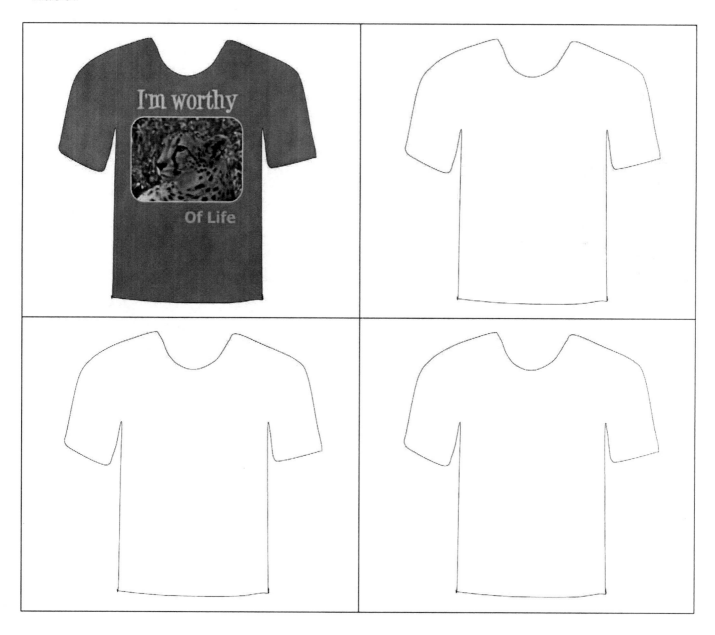

Billboard Design: This activity requires students to design a billboard along the Interstate. The following is an example of promoting tourism in New Mexico. You can change the wording of the directions to fit your classroom needs. Pick up the document in the **design** folder titled **billboard.** You can see two examples by opening the **pdf** in the **Design** folder called **billboard example.** The videos titled **autoshape tips, tracing clipart** and **t-shirts** in the **video folder** can be a general guide for designing your billboard.

Designing Billboards

Directions: You have just been hired to design a billboard along the Interstate. It can promote a variety of causes such as environmental or social awareness, anti bullying or crime, etc. It can also be for the promotion of tourism to certain geographic locations. Let your teacher give you a topic. Come up with a slogan or statement and a design for your billboard. The following are examples of what billboards might look like.

Billboard Details AutoShapes were chosen to create this billboard. All of them are the exact same size. They were even aligned along the bottom and sides to give a sense of organization. The images might have to be cropped in the same general shape as the AutoShape or you will lose quality.

Puzzle Design: This activity requires students to fill in puzzle pieces of a unit they might be working on. Each piece of the puzzle can visually represent whatever the teacher requires of them. It can be for a visual book report or representation of a state or country. The **puzzle template** can be found in the **design folder**.

Place Your Title Here

Colorado Renaissance Festival

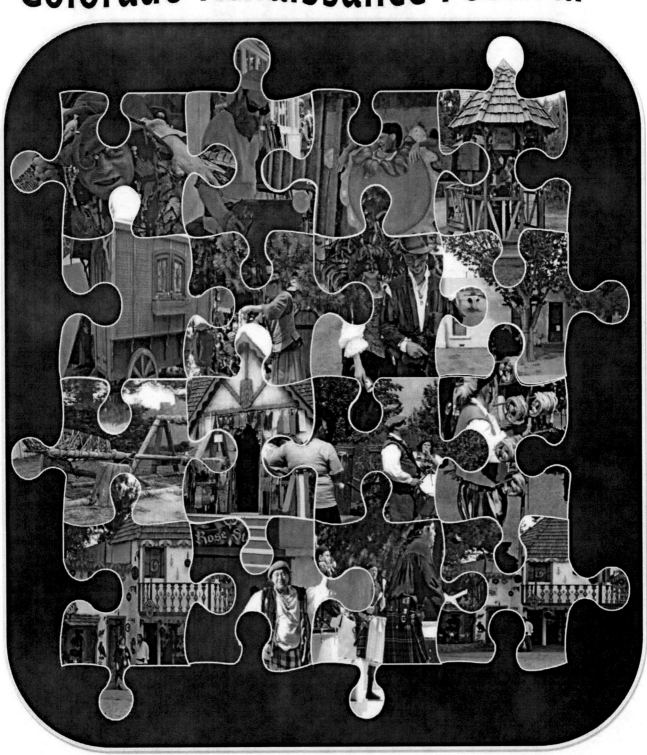

Product Design: This activity requires students to decorate the following products and provide a description that will entice others to want to purchase the product based on the description. You can watch the **product design** video in the **video folder** for tips.

Product	Description
Company Name: Cactus Juice Cafe	

Product Design Example: This is an example of what the final product might look like. Students can be creative with their design and logos. The example titled **product design example** can be picked up in the **design folder.** You can see some examples for web design: http://www.kidsnetsoft.com/html/

Product	Description
Company Name: Cactus Juice Cafe	
	This 100% cotton shirt, created in the United States, comes in a variety of sizes and colors. It is extremely comfortable and looks great with jeans. Every time you wear this shirt to our restaurant, we will give you a free round of our homemade salsa and chips. If more than one person at your table wears this shirt, our staff will sing you a song or two. For every t-shirt sold, we will give 5% to one of our local charities.
	This 20 ounce can contains our famous spicy cactus jelly. It is made with pure ingredients from local farmers. It is made on the premises of our restaurant. We pride ourselves in serving our customers quality products. We decided to create a spicy cactus jelly for all you chili lovers. We noticed that our customers were adding the jelly to some of their spicy dishes. Once you have finished this delicious jelly, you can use the glass for beverages.
	This beautiful picture, with a customized frame, will look great in any kitchen. This photo was taken by Mauricio Valenzuela, a local artist. He knows how to capture the moment with his skills as a professional photographer. Our café has been in this building since the 1960s. We were fortunate to acquire this property to create our dream café to please customers like you.
	This baseball cap has our embroidered cactus logo. It comes in all colors to compliment your wardrobe. This baseball cap can fit just about any head. It is made right here in our hometown. We like to build a strong community by supporting local artists. We donate 5% of all sales of this hat to our community center so that young people have a positive place to go.

Activity 17 Fun with Language: This section will give students a unique way of appreciating language. Activities involve a heavy emphasis on visual literacy. Through photos, students can make enhanced connections with words, leading to greater achievement, especially for those visual learners.

Idioms: This activity allows students to go online and find idioms that they want to visually represent. They are required to represent at least 10 idioms. They must give their meaning and then find an image to represent that idiom. For the next several lessons, students can incorporate these concepts in PowerPoint, Moviemaker or Photo Story. A multi media presentation might be a little more interesting. They could add music to really spice things up and then show their classmates. The document **idioms** can be picked up in the **language folder**. The **autoshape tips** video in the **video folder** will demonstrate how to add images to AutoShapes.

Directions: Fill in the table below. Use the following site to locate idioms: http://www.idiomsite.com/ If this site isn't available, Google idioms or get books from the library. Choose 10 or more idioms to visually represent. To understand how to add images to AutoShapes, watch the **autoshape tips** video. The first one is done as an example.

Idiom	Image
A picture is worth a thousand words.	
Meaning	
A visual image is more descriptive than words. Though descriptive and eloquent words could give you a general idea about the scene, I chose this image because it evoked greater feelings than words.	

Idiom	Image
Meaning	

49

Quotes: This activity allows students to go online and find quotes that they want to visually represent. They are required to represent at least 10 quotes. They must find an image to visually represent the meaning of the quote. A multi media presentation might be a little more interesting. Check out the folder titled **quotes unit.** The following document titled **quotes** can be picked up in the **language folder.**

Directions: Fill in the table below. You can use the following site to get links to various quotes based on themes: http://www.kidsnetsoft.com/html/quotes.html If necessary, you can Google quotes based on your interests. Choose 10 or more quotes to visually represent. To understand how to add images to AutoShapes, watch the **autoshape tips** video. The first two have been done as an example.

Picture	Picture
Quote and author	Quote and author
"Every day should be Earth Day." By unknown	"Take care of the earth and she will take care of you." by unknown

Picture	Picture
Quote and author	Quote and author

Ten Adjectives

Directions: Fill in the table below. Find 10 images that interest you online. To understand how to add images to AutoShapes, watch the **autoshape tips** video. For every image you add to this table, you must use 10 or more adjectives to describe the photo. You can use the built in thesaurus of Microsoft Word or search online for descriptive words. Afterwards, write two or more sentences describing the image, using three or more of the adjectives from your list. The first one is done as an example.

10 Adjectives	Picture
Old, abandoned, dilapidated, neglected, uninhabited, isolated, historical, interesting, undersized, derelict	
Sentence	
The undersized and dilapidated building was abandoned for unknown reasons. Only the last residents can fully understand why they had to leave this structure vulnerable to the unyielding forces of nature.	

10 Adjectives	Picture
Sentence	

51

Definitions: This activity requires students to define 10 or more words. For each word, they must provide an image to compliment the word and then write a sentence including that word. This document, titled **definitions**, can be found in the **language folder**.

Words Defined

Directions: Look up 10 or more words. Provide a definition for each word and then write one or more sentences that includes that word. Provide a picture to visually compliment the word . To understand how to add images to AutoShapes, watch the **autoshape tips** video. The first one is done as an example.

Word: flourish	
Definition	**Image**
To flourish is to grow and thrive. It can also mean to achieve success or to prosper.	
Sentence	
The cacti flourished beyond belief in the deserts of Mesilla, New Mexico. They were able to flourish in a climate that is ideal for a variety of cacti.	

Word:	
Definition	**Image**
Sentence	

Metaphors

Directions: Fill in the table below. Find 10 metaphors that interest you online or from books. Each metaphor must be visually represented. To understand how to add images to AutoShapes, watch the **autoshape tips** video. For every metaphor, you will provide an image and a meaning. The first one is done as an example. **Metaphor Defined:** The comparison of one thing to that of another. If you use like or as in the sentence, it is not considered a metaphor. Similes include the use of like or as and can often be confused with a metaphor. For instance, "Jimmy is a pig" is a metaphor while "Jimmy eats like a pig" is a simile.

Metaphor	Picture
The air was quiet	
Meaning	
To me, the air was quiet describes a peaceful place where it is totally silent. This picture was chosen because it seems removed from humans and their industrialized ways. There is no wind, birds or other animals to provide sounds.	

Metaphor	Picture
Meaning	

53

Similes: Students will find 10 or more similes. They will provide the simile and describe its meaning. They will also provide an image to represent the simile. This document, titled **simile**, can be found in the **language folder**.

Similes

Directions: Fill in the table below. Find 10 similes that interest you online or from books. You can even create your own. Each simile must be visually represented. To understand how to add images to AutoShapes, watch the **autoshape tips** video. For every simile, you will provide an image and a meaning. The first one is done as an example. **Simile Defined**: Similes compare two things that are usually different. For example, he eats like a pig or she is sleeping like a log. Like or as are used in sentences to make the comparisons.

Simile	Picture
It was old as the hills.	
Meaning	
When someone says something is as old as the hills, they are exaggerating that they think something is really old. The hills have been around for thousands if not millions of years, so such a comparison overstates that they think the person or object being compared is really old. Because this wagon was used before I was born, I used it to represent the simile as old as the hills.	

Simile	Picture
Meaning	

Synonyms and Antonyms

Directions: Fill in the table below. Find 10 images that interest you online. To understand how to add images to AutoShapes, watch the **autoshape tips** video. For every image you add to this table, you must use 10 or more synonyms and 10 or more antonyms to describe the photo. You can use the built in thesaurus of Microsoft Word or search online for descriptive words. The first one is done as an example.

Synonyms	Picture
Serene, peaceful, tranquil, attractive, relaxing, natural, isolated, secluded, refreshing, breath taking	
Antonyms	
Bustling, unappealing, populated, boring, earsplitting, unnatural, uninspiring, stressful, unsightly, unimpressive	

Synonyms	Picture
Antonyms	

Great resources: http://www.synonym.com/; http://www.scholastic.com/wordgirl/synonym_toast.htm; http://www.synonym.org/

55

Analogies

Directions: An analogy is the similarity between like attributes of two things by which a comparison is made. Some synonyms include likeness, similarity, comparison, and resemblance. Students can create their own analogies for this project. Choose 10 or more analogies to visually represent. To understand how to add images to AutoShapes, watch the **autoshape tips** video. The first one is done as an example.

First part of analogy	Second Part of analogy
Shack is to poverty as	mansion is to wealth.
Image representing 1st part of analogy	Image representing 2nd part of analogy

First part of analogy	Second Part of analogy
Image representing 1st part of analogy	Image representing 2nd part of analogy

> **10 Verbs** Students will get 10 images that they will provide 10 or more verbs to describe what is occurring in the photo. This document, titled **10 verbs**, can be found in the **language folder**.

10 Verbs

Directions: Fill in the table below. Find 10 images that interest you online. To understand how to add images to AutoShapes, watch the **autoshape tips** video. For every image you add to this table, you must use 10 or more verbs to describe the photo. You can use the built in thesaurus of Microsoft Word or search online for verbs. Afterwards, write two or more sentences describing the image, using three or more of the verbs from your list. The first one is done as an example.

10 Verbs	Picture
Negotiating, purchasing, dialoguing, haggling, bargaining, questioning, inquiring, desiring, yearning, convincing	
Sentence	
The well dressed couple inquired about the genuineness of the aesthetically pleasing jewelry that the woman so desperately yearned to have in her possession. After several minutes of haggling, the jeweler agreed to sell the merchandise for half his asking price. The couple's ability to negotiate paid off.	

10 Verbs	Picture
Sentence	

57

Adverbs Students will get 10 images that they will provide 10 or more adverbs to describe what is occurring in the photo. This document, titled **adverbs**, can be found in the **language folder**.

Adverbs

Directions: Fill in the table below. Find 10 images that interest you online. To understand how to add images to AutoShapes, watch the **autoshape tips** video. For every image you add to this table, you must use 5 or more verbs to describe the photo. You can use the built in thesaurus of Microsoft Word or search online for verbs. Once you have used 5 or more verbs that could describe the photo, write the combination of that verb with an adverb. Use one or more of the verb and adverbs in a sentence to describe the photo.

5 Verbs	Picture
Working; creating; designing; refining; entertaining	
5 Adverbs complimenting the 5 verbs	
Working diligently; passionately creating; creatively designing; patiently refining; knowingly entertaining	
Sentence	
The artist worked diligently on his masterpiece while knowingly entertaining his audience with his passion as a professional glass blower.	

5 Verbs	Picture
5 Adverbs complimenting the 5 verbs	
Sentence	

Activity 18 Fun with Stories: This section will give students a unique way of learning the characteristics of story writing. Everyone knows that in every story, there should be a beginning, middle and end. The following activities should contribute to a greater understanding about how to write certain aspects of a story. There needs to be focus. It has been highly recommended that the story's point of view should be written so that the character's five senses are represented. "If your reader's five senses are stimulated, you are more likely to immerse that reader in your story." The beginning is critical. The reader needs to be captivated immediately to maintain their interest. Establish the characters early on in your story. Build their personalities in such a way that the reader can visualize the characters.

Beginnings: Students will look at the first chapter of at least 5 books. They will read until they have learned about four or more characters. While reading the first chapter, they will list the traits of at least four characters mentioned in the book. This document, titled **beginning**, can be found in the **language folder**.

Title	Author	Character's Name	Character's Traits	Have you been captivated? Why or why not?
Harry Potter and the Sorcerer's Stone	J.K. Rowling	Mr. Dursley	Director of a firm, big, beefy, man with hardly any neck, very large mustache, short tempered	I was captivated by the first chapter because of how some of the main characters were described and the details of scenes. The scenes and descriptions of the characters were detailed enough to give me the imagery necessary to fully appreciate what was happening in the story. I was able to visualize the characters and the scenes.
		Mrs. Dursley	Thin, blonde, nearly twice the usual amount of neck, nosey	
		Dudley	Small son of Mr. and Mrs. Dursley, spoiled	
		Harry Potter	Famous, jet black hair, curiously shaped cut on his forehead, admired	
		Cat	Mysterious, black, clever, sneaky	

The Five Senses: Students will look at the rouhly the first chapter of at least 5 books. While reading, they are to write down every time they come across a word or phrase that describes one of the five senses. This document, titled **five senses**, can be found in the **language folder.**

Directions: It is highly recommended that descriptions in the story incorporate the character's five senses. Fill in the table below to get a general idea how published books establish the five different senses: sight, hearing, taste, touch and smell. You will need access to at least 5 books for this project. Read until you have listed at least 10 attributes of the five senses, roughly one chapter. You don't have to list all five senses, especially since the book you chose to represent might not cover all five senses within the first chapter. The first one has been done as an example so you can see what the expectations are. You might need to put them in partial phrases to be more understandable.

Title:	The Second Summer of the Sisterhood	
Author:	Ann Brashares	
Five Senses		Give some examples of how you would have written differently
Sight	Beautiful jeans; black socks; thin; muscled; tears; yellow eyelashes; hands were shaking;	I had to read several pages before being able to list all those senses. I saw many opportunities for the provision of odors to liven up the story. For this particular beginning, taste didn't seem to have much of a place at first. Hopefully, some of the other chapters will incorporate taste. I did see several opportunities for the author to embellish the story with more descriptive words. For instance, when she mentions letters received in the mail, she could have said "On the carpet lay four envelopes, with distinct smells of lavender and lilac", instead of "On the carpet lay four envelopes..." Unless of course, the author wishes to give a smell that brings disgust to the reader.
Hearing	Clacking her teeth; heart pounding; yelled; swirling the air;	
Taste		
Touch	Comforting pants; bangs her heel;	
Smell	Old sweat;	

Title:		
Author:		
Five Senses		Give some examples of how you would have written differently
Sight		
Hearing		
Taste		
Touch		
Smell		

Characters: Students will find 5 or more characters online. For every image they use for this project, they will write 5 or more sentences describing their character. The descriptions provided for each character should contribute to an interesting story that involves every character. This document, titled **characters**, can be found in the **language folder**.

Characters

Directions: Fill in the table below. Find 5 characters that interest you online. To understand how to add images to AutoShapes, watch the **autoshape tips** video. For every image you add to this table, you must write 5 or more sentences describing your character. The descriptions provided for each character should contribute to an interesting story that involves every character. The first one has been done as an example to demonstrate expectations. Write in such a way that you can visualize each character. Use actions to help the reader imagine the character and how they behave.

Descriptive sentences describing your character.	Character
Temperamental and caustic, Joey alienated his friends and family. His poor education, unstable employment and grave addictions prevented him from having a lifestyle conducive to cleanliness, comfort and security. Without a continuous flow of money, he came up with a plan that would lead him to a course of irreversible destruction. His unfortunate choices would result in unforgiving consequences.	

Descriptive sentences describing your character.	Character

Settings: Students will find 5 or more settings online. For every image they use for this project, they will write 5 or more sentences describing their setting. The descriptions provided for each setting should contribute to an interesting story that involves every setting. This document, titled **settings**, can be found in the **language folder**.

Directions: Fill in the table below. Find 5 settings that interest you online. To understand how to add images to AutoShapes, watch the **autoshape tips** video. For every image you add to this table, you must write 5 or more sentences describing your setting. The descriptions provided for each setting should contribute to an interesting story that involves every setting. The first one has been done as an example to demonstrate expectations.

Descriptive sentences describing your setting.	Setting
Samantha spent most of her day working as a waitress at the local Mexican restaurant in her hometown. She didn't mind working there because the wages sufficiently paid her bills. However, she did mind the customers who tended to be discourteous and boorish. She was able to handle her customers with her wit and confidence. Fortunately, her job was temporary because she planned on getting a career with the local newspaper once she got her Bachelor's degree in journalism.	

Descriptive sentences describing your setting.	Setting

Rising Action of a Story: Students will find 5 or more images that could represent the rising action of a story. For every image they use in this project, they will write 5 or more sentences describing the rising action of a story. The descriptions provided for each rising action should contribute to interesting stories. This document, titled **rising action**, can be found in the **language folder**.

Directions: The rising action of a story involves a series of actions, problems or complications that sets up the conflict for the main character. After tension builds, the story will eventually lead to the climax of the story. Fill in the table below. Find 5 images that could represent the rising action of a story. To understand how to add images to AutoShapes, watch the **autoshape tips** video. For every image you add to this table, you must write 5 or more sentences describing the rising action. The descriptions provided for each rising action should contribute to interesting stories. The first one has been done as an example to demonstrate expectations.

Descriptive sentences describing the rising action attributes of the story.	Image
The police had been looking for Joey since he was recently accused of committing a horrific crime. He insisted he was innocent, but the police had evidence and reason to believe that Joey was no saint. The police got a tip that Joey was working at Dante's, an Italian restaurant in downtown Denver. With this tip, they rushed to Dante's with full protection and weapons anticipating a possible deadly confrontation because Joey is known for his volatility and lack of conscience.	

Descriptive sentences describing the rising action attributes of the story.	Image

Climax of a Story: Students will find 5 or more images that could represent the climax of a story. For every image they use in this project, they will write 5 or more sentences describing the climax. The descriptions provided for each climax should contribute to interesting stories. This document, titled **climax of a story**, can be found in the **language folder**.

Directions: Climax is the high point of a story. It is usually the most exciting point of a story. Fill in the table below. Find 5 images that could represent the climax of a story. To understand how to add images to AutoShapes, watch the **autoshape tips** video. For every image you add to this table, you must write 5 or more sentences describing the climax. The descriptions provided for each climax should contribute to interesting stories. The first one has been done as an example to demonstrate expectations.

Descriptive sentences describing your climax.	Image
After searching for years, was he about to finally meet Samantha or would it be another dead end? When arriving to her supposed location, he stared at her with fear and excitement. Could this be her, he pondered? She had similar features that could easily qualify them as brother and sister. When she finished her act as a street entertainer, he approached her with reluctance. She approached him as if she knew him. She smiled and threw her arms around him crying, "we are finally together after all these years." He didn't question how she knew, he just held on to her as tight as he could with elated joy.	

Descriptive sentences describing your climax.	Image

Activity 19: Web 2.0 tools and open source. The Internet is packed with great tools for education. Web 2.0 often refers to new technology that involves mass publishing to audiences that can participate and contribute. This can be an empowering experience for students. Along with the educational value comes ethical and moral responsibilities. We not only should be encouraging our students to take part in this wonderful opportunity, but we also need to be educating them about being appropriate. This will be apparent in all lessons demonstrated. In addition to web 2.0 tools comes Open Source software. "Open Source refers to a program or software in which the source code is available to the general public for use and/or modification from its original design free of charge." webopedia Such software gives schools the opportunity to use great applications free of charge.

Resources: Many of the resources for this lesson will be posted on my website. Because many of these tools will change, this part of my website will be kept current. Some are web 2.0 tools while others are great for embellishing your content. To get the web 2.0 resources, go to: http://www.kidsnetsoft.com/html/web20.html. Many of the open source resources can be found at http://www.kidsnetsoft.com/html/open.html

Warning: Always prescreen links before showing them to your students. Web site addresses change hands. Sometimes for the worse.

- **Alice**: "Alice is an innovative 3D programming environment that makes it easy to create an animation for telling a story, playing an interactive game, or a video to share on the web."
  http://www.alice.org/

- **Any Video Converter**: Great tool for converting file types. http://www.any-video-converter.com/products/for_video_free/

- **Audacity**: "Audacity is a free, easy-to-use audio editor and recorder for Windows, Mac OS X, GNU/Linux, and other operating systems....Cut, copy, splice, and mix sounds together. Change the speed or pitch of a recording." Record voices for audio projects.
  http://audacity.sourceforge.net/

- **Animoto**: This free website will allow you to create your own videos by incorporating images, video and sound. Your final production could look like a trailer. You can e-mail to friends, post it to your site or download it to your computer. http://animoto.com/education

- **Assign-A-Day**: "Assign-A-Day is a free tool designed to enhance teacher and student communication through an online teacher-managed calendar. Teachers create a calendar for each of their classes and add assignments for the students to view. "
  http://assignaday.4teachers.org/

- **Awesome Stories**: This site is designed to help educators or individuals find original sources of information Get biographies, disasters, trials, movies, and more http://www.awesomestories.com/

- **ccMixter**: "ccMixter is a community music site featuring remixes licensed under Creative Commons where you can listen to, sample, mash-up, or interact with music in whatever way you want." http://ccmixter.org/

- **Camstudio**: "CamStudio is able to record all screen and audio activity on your computer and create industry-standard AVI video files and using its built-in SWF Producer can turn those AVIs into lean, mean, bandwidth-friendly Streaming Flash videos (SWFs)" http://camstudio.org/

- **The Citation Machine**: This site allows you to properly cite sources for projects. It allows you to type in criteria and it will generate MLA or APA citations for projects. http://citationmachine.net/index2.php?reqstyleid=2

- **Community Walk**: "CommunityWalk is a website that is dedicated to providing a powerful yet simple and easy to use interface for creating informational, interactive, and engaging maps." http://www.communitywalk.com/

- **Clear**: This site is a center for language education and research at Michigan State University. "The majority of our products are available free of charge. This includes web applications for language learning and teaching, CD-ROMs, and a variety of downloadable PDF publications." http://clear.msu.edu/clear/store/

- **Common Craft**: Common Craft has an array of videos available for people interested in learning about a variety of topics ranging from internet concepts to business. It is a great resource for teachers that want to simplify concepts that might otherwise be considered complex. Their method of instruction includes the use of video and paper to make complicated concepts easier to understand. http://www.commoncraft.com/

- **Complete Web 2.0 Directory**: This has an overwhelming number of web 2.0 sites. http://www.go2web20.net/

- **Del.icio.us:** "Keep links to your favorite articles, blogs, music, reviews, recipes, and more, and access them from any computer on the web. Share favorites with friends, family, coworkers, and the del.icio.us community." http://del.icio.us/

- **Digital Web Magazine**: This site has great resources for web users. There are articles about blogging, design and more. http://www.digital-web.com/topics/

- **ePals**: "ePals is the leading provider of school-safe collaborative learning products for K-12 across 200 countries and territories." http://www.epals.com/

- **flauntR:** "flauntR is created with the vision of enabling consumers to enhance photos or images without reading through heaps of user manuals or purchasing and downloading expensive software." http://www.flauntr.com/

- **Flickr:** Flickr allows you to manage and share your photos. Great source for using images for projects. There are great images on this site, but always check for appropriateness before sharing. http://www.flickr.com/

- **Gabcast:** Create podcasts, post audio to your blogs, host conference calls and more. http://www.gabcast.com/

- **Gcast:** This site allows you to set up an account with your cell phone and a designated pin number. Once you set up an account, you call an 800 number. Once you give your pin number associated with your phone number, you can record a message. That message will then be uploaded to your website on Gcast after pressing the pound button. There is a fee for uploading voice by phone, however, you can upload sound recordings for free. http://www.gcast.com/

- **Gimp:** "GIMP is the GNU Image Manipulation Program. It is a freely distributed piece of software for such tasks as photo retouching, image composition and image authoring. It works on many operating systems, in many languages." http://www.gimp.org/

- **Glogster:** "Mix graphics, photos, videos, music and text into slick Glogs. Glog yourself every day! Amaze your friends - send others links to your Glogs." http://www.glogster.com/edu/

- **Google Language Tools:** "Type a search phrase in your own language to easily find pages in another language. We'll translate the results for you to read." http://www.google.com/language_tools

- **Google Sketch Up:** "Google SketchUp is software that you can use to create 3D models of anything you like." http://sketchup.google.com/

- **Internet Classrooms:** This education site is packed with resources pertaining to Web 2.0 tools. http://www.internet4classrooms.com/web2.htm

- **Kathy Schrock's Guide for Educators:** This site has a variety of resources for teachers. Don't miss "The Icing on the Cake Online Tools for Classroom Use" http://school.discoveryeducation.com/schrockguide/edtools.html

- **Librivox:** "LibriVox provides free audiobooks from the public domain. There are several options for listening." http://librivox.org/

- **Mastery Maze:** "The goal of this site is to combine content management with a little social networking to create a space on the web where teachers and students can work together to achieve

- **NVU**: NVU is a complete web authoring tool in the open source community. http://net2.com/nvu

- **Open Office**: "OpenOffice.org is a multiplatform and multilingual office suite and an open-source project. Compatible with all other major office suites, the product is free to download, use, and distribute." http://www.openoffice.org/

- **Page Flakes:** Pageflakes is a free online tool that will allow users to create and organize a newspaper style website. They can select news topics that interest them. They can drag and drop stories wherever they want on the page. Users are able to change the newspaper or other interested sites that have rss feeds. I can't wait to explore and possibly incorporate this into my curriculum. http://www.pageflakes.com/

- **Paint.net**: "Paint.NET is free image and photo editing software for computers that run Windows. It features an intuitive and innovative user interface with support for layers, unlimited undo, special effects, and a wide variety of useful and powerful tools." http://www.getpaint.net/

- **PDF Online**: This site will allow you to convert documents to PDFs for free. http://www.pdfonline.com/

- **Photoshop Express**: This site lets you manipulate and store images for free. https://www.photoshop.com/

- **Plagiarism Checker**: Check for plagiarism. http://www.dustball.com/cs/plagiarism.checker/

- **PB Wiki**: Create wikis for the classroom for free. http://pbworks.com/

- **Puzzle Maker:** This site allows you to create a variety of puzzles for your classroom. http://puzzlemaker.discoveryeducation.com/

- **Remix America:** "RemixAmerica.org is a multi-partisan, non-profit website that uses digital technology to give everyone the chance to own the words, the music, the images and sounds of America in digital form; to remix those expressions and ideas with their own; and to send the products of our community's creativity out to the world... where others will come back to us and start it all over again..." http://www.remixamerica.org/

- **Scratch**: "Scratch is designed to help young people (ages 8 and up) develop 21st century learning skills. As they create and share Scratch projects, young people learn important mathematical and computational ideas, while also learning to think creatively, reason systematically, and work collaboratively." http://scratch.mit.edu/

- **Screen Toaster:** This is a free tool that allows you to capture videos of onscreen action with one click. You can register and use it anywhere and anytime. "Record screencasts, tutorials, demos, training, lectures and more." http://www.screentoaster.com/

- **Scribd**: "Today, Scribd is the largest social publishing company in the world — the website where more than 60 million people each month discover and share original writings and documents." http://www.scribd.com/

- **Senduit**: Senduit is an easy way to send files. You can upload a file to be retrieved at a temporary website provided by the services of this website. You can retrieve your uploaded files up to seven days. This would be a great way for students to upload files to be retrieved at home or at school. You can send up to 100 MB. http://www.senduit.com/

- **ShowBeyond**: This site allows you to create a slide presentation and record a message to be associated with the photo. http://www.showbeyond.com/show/home

- **Skype**: Skype is a free software that lets you talk over the Internet to anyone, anywhere in the world. Use Skype to chat with up to 100 people in a group chat. http://www.skype.com/

- **Snipshot**: This website allows you to upload images from your computer for editing purposes. You can even enter a Web address of any photo stored online and get a copy with which to work. The site will keep a copy of the uploaded image for 24 hours before they get rid of it. http://snipshot.com/

- **Sound Transit**: "SoundTransit is a collaborative, online community dedicated to field recording and phonography. On this site, you can plan a sonic journey through various locations recorded around the world, or you can search the database for specific sounds by different artists from certain places." http://soundtransit.nl/

- **Teacher Tube:** Get video and photos for classroom learning. You can upload your photos and video to Teacher Tube. http://www.teachertube.com/

- **TimeRime**: "TimeRime.com is an online community that allows people to create, compare and upload information by creating timelines." http://timerime.com/

- **Tumblr**: "Effortlessly share text, photos, quotes, links, music, and videos from your computer or phone." http://www.tumblr.com/

- **Tux Paint**: "Tux Paint is a free, award-winning drawing program for children ages 3 to 12 (preschool and K-6). It combines an easy-to-use interface, fun sound effects, and an encouraging cartoon mascot who guides children as they use the program." http://tuxpaint.org/

- **Twitter**: "Twitter is a service for friends, family, and co-workers to communicate and stay connected through the exchange of quick, frequent answers to one simple question: What are you doing?" http://twitter.com/

- **280 Slides**: "Create beautiful presentations, access them from anywhere, and share them with the world. With 280 Slides, there's no software to download and nothing to pay for – and when you're done building your presentation you can share it any way you like." http://280slides.com/

- **Ustream.TV**: Ustream TV allows you to easily broadcast your multimedia productions. You can create your own channel. http://www.ustream.tv/

- **Virsona**: Virsona is a unique "Online Community," that gives you the ability to create, store and then interact with the entirety of your life experiences. You can ask questions of famous people. If they answer incorrectly or if they don't know the answer, you can teach them. It will be evaluated by the founder and updated if appropriate. http://www.virsona.com/

- **VoiceThread**:"A VoiceThread is an online media album that can hold essentially any type of media (images, documents and videos) and allows people to make comments in 5 different ways - using voice (with a microphone or telephone), text, audio file, or video (with a webcam) - and share them with anyone they wish." http://voicethread.com/

- **WikiSpaces**: WikiSpaces allows you to set up a wiki. You can control who sees and edits your pages. You can link to great resources for projects, imbed videos to enhance your curriculum and more. http://www.wikispaces.com/

- **WizIQ**: "WiZiQ brings students and teachers together regardless of the boundaries. With absolutely no cost to join or use its state-of-the-art virtual classroom, WiZiQ is becoming a vital tool in an online teacher's or a student's toolkit." http://www.wiziq.com/

- **Wordle**: "Wordle is a toy for generating "word clouds" from text that you provide. The clouds give greater prominence to words that appear more frequently in the source text. You can tweak your clouds with different fonts, layouts, and color schemes. The images you create with Wordle are yours to use however you like. You can print them out, or save them to the Wordle gallery to share with your friends." http://www.wordle.net/

- **Word Press:** "**WordPress** is a state-of-the-art publishing platform with a focus on aesthetics, web standards, and usability. WordPress is both free and priceless at the same time." http://wordpress.org/

- **Yodio**: You can add your voice to digital photos for free. http://www.yodio.com/

- **Zamzar**: Zamzar is a free online resource that will convert between various file types. For example, if you have sound that is a wave and you need to convert it to an mp3, you can do that on this site. http://www.zamzar.com/

- **Zoho Notebook**: This website allows users to freely set up an account in order to put content, images, audio and video online. You can grant reading and writing permissions to online viewers. http://notebook.zoho.com/

- **Be Funky:** "Turn your photos into incredible artwork with one click"
  http://www.befunky.com/

- **Blabberize**: This site allows you to upload an image and your voice. The image will then move its mouth with your story. http://blabberize.com/

- **Color Scheme Designer:** Need some color schemes that work, check out this site. It provides a variety of color schemes for web design and more. http://colorschemedesigner.com/

- **Edheads:** "Edheads helps students learn through educational games and activities designed to meet state and national standards." You can perform a virtual hip replacement, knee surgery or hip resurfacing. This site is really awesome! http://www.edheads.org/

- **Elbot**: Talk to Elbot, a friendly robot. Don't say mean things to it, it is very sensitive. Besides, it isn't nice to be mean to anyone, even a robot. http://www.elbot.com/

- **Exploratorium**: Exploratorium has a wealth of resources. Their site claims to have over 18 thousand award winning Web Pages that explore hundreds of different topics.
  http://www.exploratorium.edu/

- **FotoFlexer**: This is a great tool for students to transform images. You can resize images, add animations and more. This is great, especially for people that don't have image editing software. http://fotoflexer.com/

- **Free Poverty:** This site gives cups of water for getting answers correct on world geography. http://www.freepoverty.com/

- **Free Rice**: This site allows you to improve your vocabulary, foreign languages and more while you give 10 grains of rice to the poor each time you get an answer correct. http://www.freerice.com/

- **Inspirational Videos**: These video resources are very profound and inspiring. Great for motivating staff and students. http://www.kidsnetsoft.com/html/inspirational.html

- **ISTE**: ISTE is the International Society for Technology in Education. This site is rich with resources for the use of technology in the classroom. http://www.iste.org/

- **Miniature Earth**: This is a short movie that gives the audience a general idea about various statistics regarding people on earth. It simplifies statistics based on the earth consisting of 100 people. http://www.miniature-earth.com/me_english.htm

- **Rate my Doodle**: "This site allows you to create animations with tools and different colors. The movie you create contain up to 500 frames. "http://www.ratemydoodle.com/doodle/make-movie

Resources: Continuation of additional resources for education and fun!

- **Planet Photoshop**: This site has a variety of resources. They offer tutorials in video format. Great site. The only dilemma is there are ads to pay for the site. Get past the ads and learn some great tools. http://www.planetphotoshop.com/tutorials.html

- **Rate my Doodle**: "This site allows you to create animations with tools and different colors. The movie you create contain up to 500 frames. "http://www.ratemydoodle.com/doodle/make-movie

- **Rethinking Schools**: This wonderful site offers a geography challenge on the Middle East. You can test your knowledge on a new drag-and-drop challenge. http://www.rethinkingschools.org/just_fun/index.shtml

- **Shambles**: This site is packed with resources for teachers. http://www.shambles.net/pages/school/

- **Stories for Change**: this site allows you to watch a variety of stories on video. You can also upload your stories to this site once you register. http://storiesforchange.net/

- **Text-Image.com**: This site lets you manipulate images without having to download software. The results are rather interesting. http://www.text-image.com/

- **3D Text Maker**: Type in a title or word and apply interesting 3D effects to your words. http://www.3dtextmaker.com/image_editor.html

- **U.S. Map Test.** This is a great review for students to test their knowledge of locating all 50 states. http://www.pibmug.com/files/map_test.swf

- **Visuwords**: Look up words on this site to find their meanings and their associations with other words. It could be considered a dictionary and a thesaurus. http://www.visuwords.com

- **Wacky Web Tales**: this site lets you choose from a variety of story options. You type in various parts of speech and then generate a story with your words. http://www.eduplace.com/tales/

- **Xtranormal**:"Xtranormal's mission is to bring movie-making to the people. Everyone watches movies and we believe everyone can make movies. Movie-making, short and long, online and on-screen, private and public, will be the most important communications process of the 21st century. http://www.xtranormal.com/

Flexible Resources: With anything related to technology, these sites are subject to change. You can access my resource page that will keep many of these tools up to date. http://www.kidsnetsoft.com/html/web20.html

Glogster: Glogster is a free online tool that allows you to add video, sound, text and images to visually and orally represent projects. It can be used for a multitude of projects. For example, visual book reports, cultural representations, historical timelines, inventions, current events, virtual posters and so much more. The following handout is an example of an organizational tool with tips on how to create a Glog. You can pick up **glog organizer,** as a word document, in the **web 2.0 folder.**

Glog Organizer

Directions: It is always great to have a plan prior to getting involved in projects. The following steps should help you be organized for this project.

1. Come up with a theme to represent on your Glog.
2. Create a folder in a safe location on your computer and name it according to your theme.
3. Determine where and how you are going to incorporate video, especially if you don't have YouTube access.
4. Determine what sounds, images and information you will use on your Glog and record the information on the table below. Be sure to paste the website address in the sources column.
5. Findsounds: http://www.findsounds.com/ is a great place to get a variety of sounds. To save a sound, right click on the sound icon and choose **Save | Target As** from the drop down menu.
6. Save the sound in your main folder that you created in step two.
7. Save large images for your project in the same folder. To save images, Pics4learning and Geek Philosopher are copyright friendly images for school projects. http://www.pics4learning.com/ ; http://geekphilosopher.com/MainPage/photos.htm

Theme:	
Images, sound, video, information	Website source

Glogster for Teachers: You can pick up the handout **glogster for teachers** as a PDF in the **web 2.0 folder.** It is essential that the teacher set up this account and create their own Glog before having their students create a Glog.

Glogster for Teachers

Directions: Go to http://www.glogster.com/edu/ and complete the following steps to create a Glog about a meaningful theme. Keep in mind that when this tutorial reflects how Glogster was set up at the time. Having no control of how their webmaster designs the site, the lesson may not represent how the site looks when you want to use this lesson.

1. When the Glogster page opens, click on the Register link. There are several locations to register.

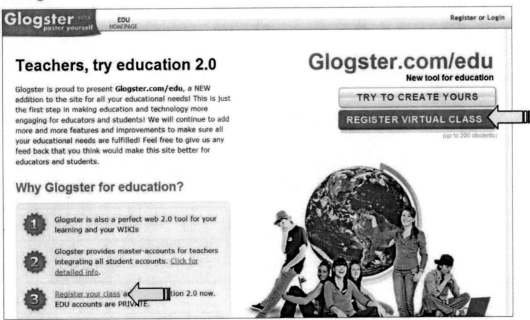

2. Register your class. Fill in the fields indicated on this page. Choose the number of students you plan on giving accounts to. In this example, I put 100 for the number of students to receive an account. You can assign as much as 200.

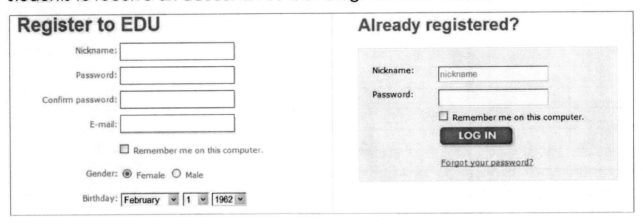

Glogster for Students

Directions: Go to http://www.glogster.com/edu/ and complete the following steps to create a Glog about a meaningful theme.

1. When the Glogster page opens, click on the **Login** link. Don't register.

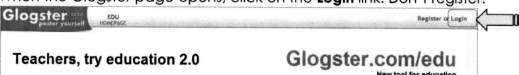

2. Login in with your assigned username and password.

Get your username and password from your teacher. Don't forget to change your password!

3. After logging in, you should get a window like this: You can say something in the **Enter your mood** talking bubble. Be nice, your peers and teacher can see what you say!

4. Click on the (**Edit your account**) link.

5. You can change your gender, birth date, name, address, etc in the **Settings** window. You should minimize information on this page. Don't add your last name or address. Be sure to click on the **Save Your Profile** button when you are done.

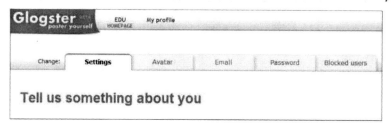

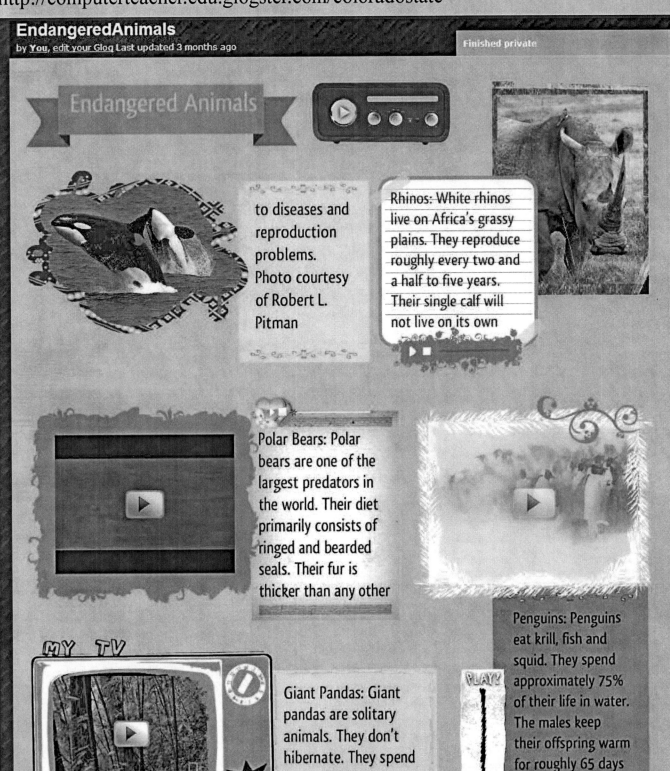

EndangeredAnimals
by **You**, edit your Glog Last updated 3 months ago

Finished private

Endangered Animals

to diseases and reproduction problems. Photo courtesy of Robert L. Pitman

Rhinos: White rhinos live on Africa's grassy plains. They reproduce roughly every two and a half to five years. Their single calf will not live on its own

Polar Bears: Polar bears are one of the largest predators in the world. Their diet primarily consists of ringed and bearded seals. Their fur is thicker than any other

Penguins: Penguins eat krill, fish and squid. They spend approximately 75% of their life in water. The males keep their offspring warm for roughly 65 days

MY TV

Giant Pandas: Giant pandas are solitary animals. They don't hibernate. They spend most of their day eating. They are

Animoto: You can pick up the PDF titled **Animoto** in the **web 2.0 folder**. Animoto is a wonderful tool that allows you to put together a 30 second video with 3 simple steps. It is free and definitely worth exploring.

1. Apply for unlimited videos for you and your students: http://animoto.com/education
2. Animoto will send you a classroom code necessary for getting started.
3. The e-mail with the classroom code should send you to the getting started page: http://animoto.com/education/getting_started
4. You should then be prompted to sign up: https://animoto.com/sign_up
5. Once you register your class, login at http://animoto.com/ Don't forget to put in your classroom code in the "Promo/Referral Code" section
6. When going to the Animoto site, you can get started putting together videos.
7. If you have no videos, the screen might say "Looks like you don't have any videos yet. **Create One.**
8. Click on the **Create One** link. You should get a window indicating you are on step one. You are to choose between an animoto short or a full length video. The animoto short is for 30 seconds and it is free of charge. Full length videos cost money.

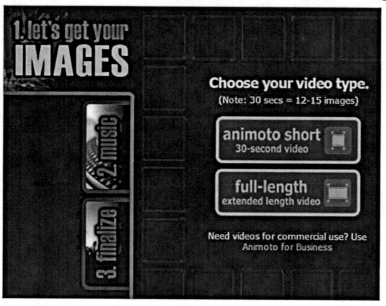 

9. Click on the animoto short unless you have paid for full length videos.
10. You can get your images by uploading them from your computer, retrieving them from another site or selecting them from animoto's collection.

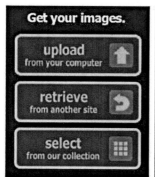

In this example, images of roughly the same size will be saved in a folder to be uploaded. If you know how to resize images, it is recommended you do so. Animoto recommends getting 12-15 images at roughly 640 X 480 pixels.

Example: You can embed Animoto movies into your web page. You can upload them to Youtube. There is also an opportunity to put them on Twitter, Facebook and more.

Kidsnetsoft *Lessons and Products*

Home
Photoshop
Publisher
Word
PowerPoint
Google
Extras
Products
Comments
About

Animoto Example

ANIMOTO

01:52

Examples of what you can do once your video is created.

DOWNLOADS

1-click Remix
Remix into a new video

Edit
Edit this video project

New
Start a new video

Delete
Delete this video

Share
Send to your contacts

Embed
Put on your blog/website

Export
Send to
YouTube/SmugMug

Web Quality

MP4 (10.88 MB)
Download

High Resolution
You have 1 hi-res upgrade
credits. Click to start rendering.

Hi-Res Upgrade

DVD Orders
Order a physical DVD.

VoiceThread: VoiceThread is a great tool for collaborating with people. You can create multimedia presentations that incorporate video, images and sound. Tell your story with your images, video and voice. Prior to getting started, it is recommended that you prepare before creating your presentation. You can pick up the **VoiceThread prep** document in the **web 2.0 folder**.

Directions: This document will help you create your presentation with ease when setting up your VoiceThread presentation. If getting images from an online source, document where you are getting your image. Since this is being published online, you need to get copyright friendly images. The public domain is one of the best places to get images. If you are providing the images, put self in the source column. For every image that you plan on using for this presentation, type in the exact name and script for each image. To add another row, click in the last row, last column and click on the Tab key of your keyboard. The first one has been done as an example.

Image Name	Script for image	Website source
festival2	The Colorado Renaissance Festival is an exciting event that has been taking place in Colorado for over 30 years. Visitors and workers alike dress in some of the most colorful and exciting clothing. Every one of your five senses will be stimulated at this festival.	self

1. Go to VoiceThread: http://voicethread.com/#home
2. Click on the register link.

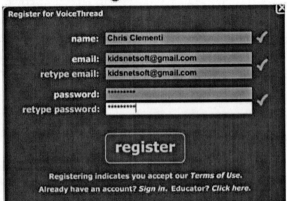

3. When you are signed in, you can click on **MyVoice** to access videos that demonstrate how to use VoiceThread. You can get the latest news and features. There are also links to VoiceThread solutions and help. The videos are very helpful.

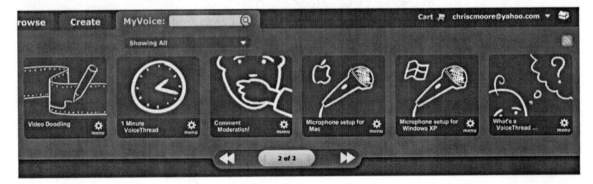

4. **Video Doodling** allows you to record everything you do while watching a video. You can pause and make comments throughout the video. You can get a helpful video on how to do this by clicking on the Video Doodling option under MyVoice. When you are done watching each video, click on the x in the upper right hand corner to get back to main menu.

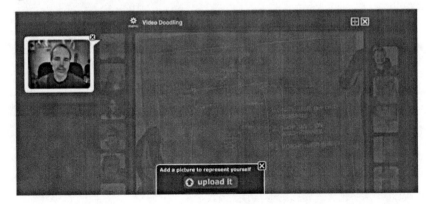

Downloading GIMP: Gimp is an image editing program that is available as Open Source. You can do a variety of image manipulations using this free software. Some say it is comparable to Photoshop. The following is an example of page one of the handout that demonstrates how to download Gimp. Before you get excited about using this in the classroom, be sure your district will allow you to install it on your computers. This handout, titled **GIMP Download**, can be found in the **open source folder.**

Directions for Downloading GIMP: Follow the steps below to download GIMP onto your computer. If you want a download of the tutorial, visit:

Go to http://www.gimp.org/windows/ if you are installing on a Windows
Go to http://www.gimp.org/macintosh/ if you are installing on a Mac
Go to http://www.gimp.org/unix/ if you are using Unix

1. The following site was accessed to download for a windows platform: http://gimp-win.sourceforge.net/stable.html Once at this site, click on the download option. Be sure you choose the correct operating system platform.

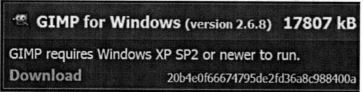

2. If it doesn't download, click on the link that says "direct link"

3. When the **File Download** window appears, click on the **Run** button.

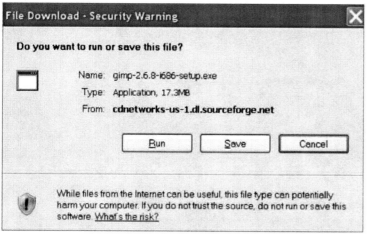

Resizing Images in GIMP This lesson will demonstrate how to resize images in GIMP. Resizing images is essential for web design. Large images can load very slow on the Internet resulting in visitors leaving the site prematurely. This lesson also demonstrates how to make images the same size for gallery pages. You can pick up **resizing images in gimp** in the **open source folder.**

Directions: This lesson will give step by step instructions on resizing images using GIMP.

1. Open up GIMP by going to **Start | All Programs | GIMP | GIMP 2**
2. The following windows should pop up with helpful windows that are part of GIMP. You can get many tips by clicking **Next Tip** in the **GIMP Tip of the Day** window. The other window has a variety of tools that you will need to manipulate images.

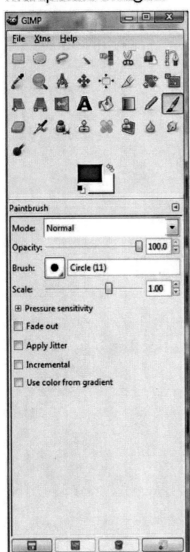

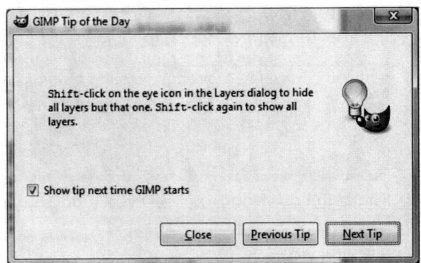

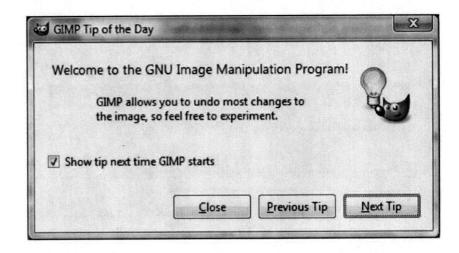

3. In order to resize your images, you can either copy and paste them directly from a website into GIMP or you can save them in your folder. Keep in mind

Downloading Paint.NET: Paint.NET is an image editing program that is available as Open Source. You can do a variety of image manipulations using this free software. The following is an example of page one of the handout that demonstrates how to download Paint.NET. Before you get excited about using this in the classroom, be sure your district will allow you to install it on your computers. This handout, titled **Paint.NET Download**, can be found in the **open source folder.**

Downloading Paint.net, a free image editing program

Directions: Follow these steps to download onto your computer.

1. Go to http://www.getpaint.net/download.html
2. Take note of the minimum system requirements.

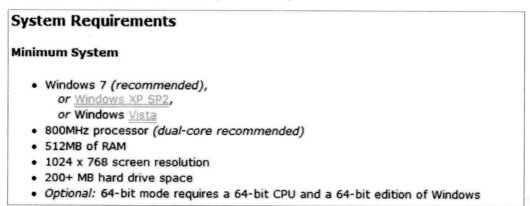

3. Locate the correct download option and click on it. Keep in mind that the façade may change, depending on when you download Pain.net

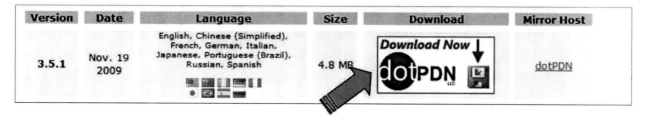

4. Locate the **Free Download Now** option and click on the link.

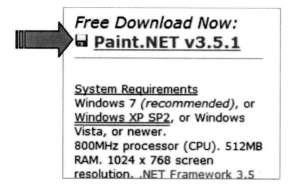

Resizing Images in Paint.NET: This lesson will demonstrate how to resize images in Paint.NET. Resizing images is essential for web design. Large images can load very slow on the Internet resulting in visitors leaving the site prematurely. This lesson also demonstrates how to make images the same size for gallery pages. You can pick up **resizing images in paint** in the **open source folder.**

Directions: the following steps will help students resize images the same size to make their final products look more professional.

1. Open up Paint.NET by going to **Start | All Programs | Paint.NET**
2. The following window should pop up with helpful windows that are part of Paint.NET.

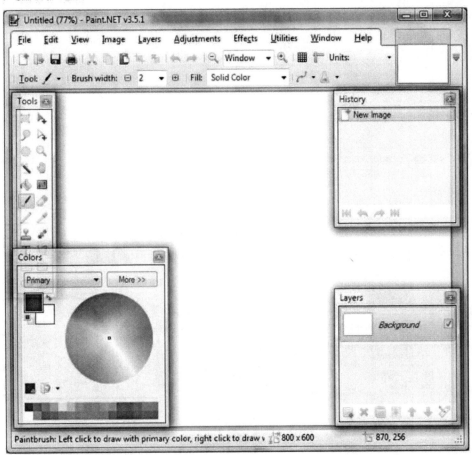

3. If you need to access the different helpful windows in Paint.NET, select **Window** from the main menu. The purpose of these windows will become clear.

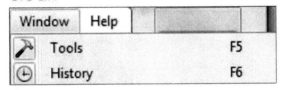

Activity 20: (Web Development) This section will give some general ideas and understandings about web development and design. There are so many possible ways students can create websites. There are resources that allow you to create sites for free. This page will give you some general resources to explore. This book also has a very user friendly handout on how to make websites using Google Sites. That is available in the Google folder.

The pages that follow will give you resources and ideas for web development. NVU is a free web authoring program that will allow your students to make sites from scratch. The only dilemma is where and how to host them. I post my students sites on my classroom website using Yahoo services. I also had to purchase my domain name Kidsnetsoft from Network Solutions. Though students can create websites using free online resources, creating them using a web authoring tool gives them a better understanding of how websites are created. I could easily use free online tools for my classroom website. The problem, however, is I wouldn't have the same control and flexibility of creating a website from scratch. When my students create websites, they have to master their organization skills in order to have a site that works. If they don't master their organization skills, they will have links that don't work and broken images.

Free Online Website Tools: These are just a few of the many services available for free websites. To get more, just Google free websites.

Open Source Templates: http://opensourcetemplates.org/: Get free attractive website templates. They offer a variety of free tools to make your life easier.

Webs.com: http://www.webs.com/: Create your own website for free. There website builder allows you to make professional looking sites.

Weebly.com: http://www.weebly.com/: You can create a free website & blog. It is relatively easy with its drag and drop interface.

Wix.com: http://www.wix.com/: This site allows you to create Flash websites for free. You can customize 100s of free Flash templates or create your own.

Yola.com: http://www.yola.com/: You can build a professional looking website using Yola services. You can get it for free or pay a minimal annual fee.

NVU NVU is a web authoring program that is available as Open Source. You can create simple web pages using this free software. The following is an example of page one of the handout that demonstrates how to download NVU. Before you get excited about using this in the classroom, be sure your district will allow you to install it on your computers. This handout, titled **NVU Download**, can be found in the **open source folder.**

Downloading NVU

1. Go to http://net2.com/nvu/download.html
2. Depending on your operating system, choose the correct download option.

DOWNLOAD NVU

Microsoft Windows - Full Installer (.exe)
This executable will install Nvu on a windows platform and integrate the software into the operating system shell (start menu, desktop icons, quick launch etc.). It is ideal for users who wish to associate system html files with an editor of choice.
Download

Microsoft Windows - Zip Version (.zip)
The Zip version can be downloaded if you are behind a restrictive firewall which blocks .exe files. The zip file can be extracted to a folder on the desktop once downloaded, and the program can then be launched from within this folder without any installation. This version does not integrate with the windows system shell.
Download

Apple Mac Disk Image (.dmg.zip)
The Macintosh Disc Image requires Mac OS X 10.1.5 or more recent. Simply download and open the image from the desktop. Drag the application icon into the Application folder under the Macintosh hard drive. This "installs" Nvu on your Mac.
Download

3. When the following window pops up, click **Run**.

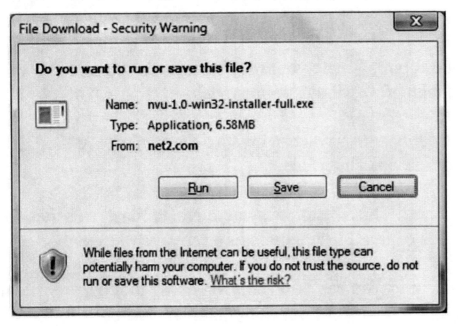

Planning a website: Students need to plan their website before diving into NVU or other web authoring programs. This could be used as a plan for a variety of themed websites. My students have made sites about hypothetical countries, museums or businesses. Some of the main sites they created had the following links, depending on what their site was about: attractions; culture; souvenirs; shopping; hotels; fans; contact; testimonies; exhibits; restaurants; etc. Pick up **website plans** in the **web development folder.**

Come up with four other possible links for your website. You will have a home page that describes your website. For each page that you come up with, provide a brief description of what will be on those pages. Title each page with as few letters as possible. For example, if you want to name the pages Places to Visit, name it Attractions.

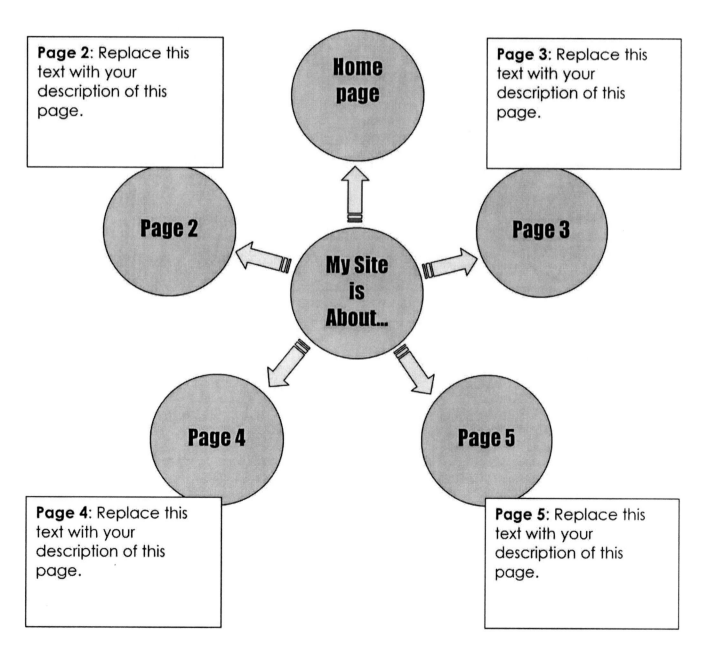

Page 2: Replace this text with your description of this page.

Home page

Page 3: Replace this text with your description of this page.

Page 2

Page 3

My Site is About...

Page 4

Page 5

Page 4: Replace this text with your description of this page.

Page 5: Replace this text with your description of this page.

Planning Your Website

Directions: Each website will have a home page that introduces the website. Use the diagram below to help organize your site. Page A- Page E will be your 5 major links. If there are subcategories, replace the subcategory word with the subcategory of that particular page. Don't feel obligated to have subcategories. Sometimes a one page write-up is sufficient for a web page. Once you have determined your main links, type their names in the navigation scheme.

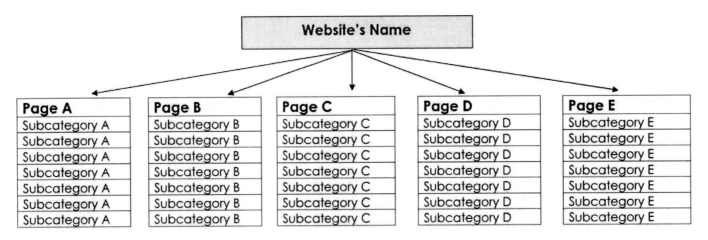

Navigation Scheme

Home	Page A	Page B	Page C	Page D	Page E

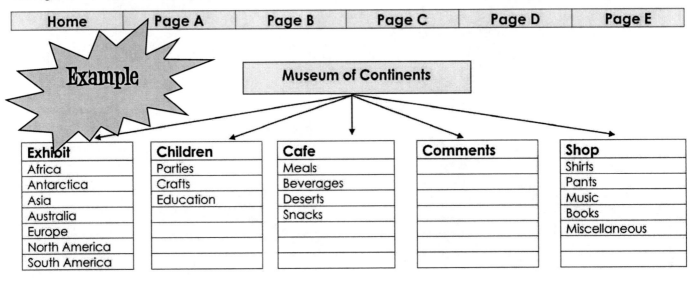

Navigation Scheme

Home	Exhibit	Children	Cafe	Comments	Store

Website Rubric This rubric can be customized for your own classroom expectations. The rubric has been created based on researching various web design sites. You can pick up the **website rubric** in the in the **web development folder.**

Criteria for building a website: Total possible points=280. Eighty possible points will be given for addressing the rubrics below: (40 points * 5 (webpages)=200) + (8 * 10=80) meeting all the following criteria.

CATEGORY	Points: 7-8	Points: 5-6	Points: 3-4	Points: 0-2
Navigation	Links for navigation are clearly labeled, consistently placed, and allow the reader to easily move from a page to related pages (forward and back), and take the reader where s/he expects to go. A user does not become lost.	Links for navigation are clearly labeled, allow the reader to easily move from a page to related pages (forward and back), and internal links take the reader where s/he expects to go. A user rarely becomes lost.	Links for navigation take the reader where s/he expects to go, but some needed links seem to be missing. A user sometimes gets lost.	Some links do not take the reader to the sites described. A user typically feels lost.
Background	Background is exceptionally attractive, consistent across pages, adds to the theme or purpose of the site, and does not detract from readability.	Background is attractive, consistent across pages, adds to the theme or purpose of the site, and does not detract from readability.	Background is consistent across pages and does not detract from readability.	Background detracts from the readability of the site.
Color Choices	Colors of background, fonts, and unvisited and visited links form a pleasing palette, do not detract from the content, and are consistent across pages.	Colors of background, fonts, and unvisited and visited links do not detract from the content, and are consistent across pages.	Colors of background, fonts, and unvisited and visited links do not detract from the content.	Colors of background, fonts, and unvisited and visited links make the content hard to read or otherwise distract the reader.
Graphics	Graphics are related to the theme/purpose of the site, are thoughtfully cropped, are of high quality and enhance reader interest or understanding.	Graphics are related to the theme/purpose of the site, are of good quality and enhance reader interest or understanding.	Graphics are related to the theme/purpose of the site, and are of good quality.	Graphics seem randomly chosen, are of low quality, OR distract the reader.

Copyright	Fair use guidelines are followed with clear, easy-to-locate and accurate citations for all borrowed material. No material is included from Web sites that state that permission is required unless permission has been obtained.	Fair use guidelines are followed with clear, easy-to-locate and accurate citations for almost all borrowed material. No material is included from Web sites that state that permission is required unless permission has been obtained.	Fair use guidelines are followed with clear, easy-to-locate and accurate citations for most borrowed material. No material is included from Web sites that state that permission is required unless permission has been obtained.	Borrowed materials are not properly documented OR material was borrowed without permission from a site that requires permission
Content	The site has a well-stated clear purpose and theme that is carried out throughout the site.	The site has a clearly stated purpose and theme, but may have one or two elements that do not seem to be related to it.	The purpose and theme of the site is somewhat muddy or vague.	The site lacks a purpose and theme.
Work Ethic	Student always uses classroom project time well. Conversations are primarily focused on the project and things needed to get the work done and are held in a manner that typically does not disrupt others.	Student usually uses classroom project time well. Most conversations are focused on the project and things needed to get the work done and are held in a manner that typically does not disrupt others.	Student usually uses classroom project time well, but occasionally distracts others from their work.	Student does not use classroom project time well OR typically is disruptive to the work of others.
Content Accuracy This only applies to non-fiction sites	All information provided by the student on the Web site is accurate and all the requirements of the assignment have been met.	Almost all the information provided by the student on the Web site is accurate and all requirements of the assignment have been met.	Almost all of the information provided by the student on the Web site is accurate and almost all of the requirements have been met.	There are several inaccuracies in the content provided by the students OR many of the requirements were not met.
Links (content)	All links point to high quality, up-to-date, credible sites.	Almost all links point to high quality, up-to-date, credible sites.	Most links point to high quality, up-to-date, credible sites.	Less than 3/4 of the links point to high quality, up-to-date, credible sites.

I'm getting an A!

Home Page Write-Up

Directions: Type up your home page of the website. You need 200 or more words. The following is an example of how your home page might look:

Example Welcome to the Museum of Strange Creatures. This museum is like no other. We are excited to share some of the most fascinating creatures that have been discovered in various parts of the world. Scientists are still dumb founded by these discoveries that have occurred in this century. We have professionals that continue to locate new creatures that became extinct more than a million years ago. With significant data, we have been able to draw scientific conclusions about these animals diet, habitat, characteristics, and more. Come to this wonderful museum and learn about the past of this incredible planet. Our museum offers recreations of strange creatures. You can visit our exhibit's page and learn about the unique creatures that inhabit different parts of our globe. Our café is definitely worth visiting. My personal favorite is the scorpions on a stick. I would recommend the strawberry cockroach shake. If you have children, I highly suggest you visit our kid's section. You can dress up like one of the animals, read books or do arts and crafts. Overall, this is one of the best museums in the world. If you want to learn and have a great time, visit the Museum of Strange Creatures.

Student Homepage: Type your homepage in the space below. Word count should be over 200 words.

Example: You can check out my museum example by visiting: http://www.kidsnetsoft.com/museum. The write-up isn't as extensive because I added an Animoto video to liven up the page.

Check out my country site: http://www.kidsnetsoft.com/chris_country

Contact/Comments Write-Up

Directions: Type in the name of the image in column one and write 100 words or more to describe the picture for your contact or comment's page. An example has been provided to clarify your understanding. You need 4 or more for your contact or comment's page.

Pictures Name	Write up for contact page
shack	This is my humble dwelling. I was able to construct this home in one day. As you can see it needs some construction. I have lived in this home since I was 25. I am waiting to make a decent salary from my ability to make outstanding websites so that I can buy a larger and more comfortable home. Unfortunately, I live in a very dangerous neighborhood with more problems than you could possibly imagine. I am often afraid to leave my home at night. If you pay me, I can move from this horrid place. Please, if you have any conscience, donate to my cause. It is worthy.
Example	

 This is one of the most fantastic and fascinating museums I have ever been to. At first I thought it was a joke, but then I read some of the Archaeologist credentials and became totally convinced of the credibility of these creatures. My favorite creature is the Biger because I like strong animals. I really enjoyed the cockroach shake. I prefer the chocolate flavor to all the others. I am a little apprehensive to try the skewered scorpions. I might get convinced to try it on another visit.

NVU NVU is an web authoring program that is available as Open Source. You can create simple web pages using this free software. The following is an example of page one of the handout that demonstrates how to create a simple web page using NVU. Before you get excited about using this in the classroom, be sure your district will allow you to install it on your computers. This handout, titled **NVU**, can be found in the **open source folder.**

1. Open up **My Computer** on the desktop.
2. Locate a safe and logical location to save your material.
3. Create a **new folder** and name it with your first name followed by an underscore. After the underscore, place the first initial of last first name. For instance, if your name is Joe Smith, you would name the folder joe_s. This will be known as your website folder.
4. Open up your website folder and create two additional folders to contain images intended for your website. Name one folder **images** and name the other folder **Photoshop** or **Gimp**, depending on which image editing program you plan on using. The **images** folder will contain all images that are prepared for your website. The Photoshop or Gimp folder will contain all images that need to be prepared for your website. This is for organizational purposes.

Creating your template page in NVU:

5. Choose **Start | All Programs | Nvu | Nvu**
6. When the following window appears, you can choose to get tips on Nvu or close the window and begin.

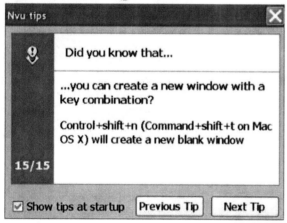

7. Save the web page before beginning. Choose **File | Save As** from the main menu. When the following window pops up, type in template.

NVU The following is an example of setting up a gallery page for a website. The NVU handout demonstrates how to make a gallery type page. To resize images the same size, check out the handouts for **Paint.NET** (Windows) or **GIMP** (Windows, Mac, Linux) which is available in the **open source folder**. It is important to make the website presentable and efficient.

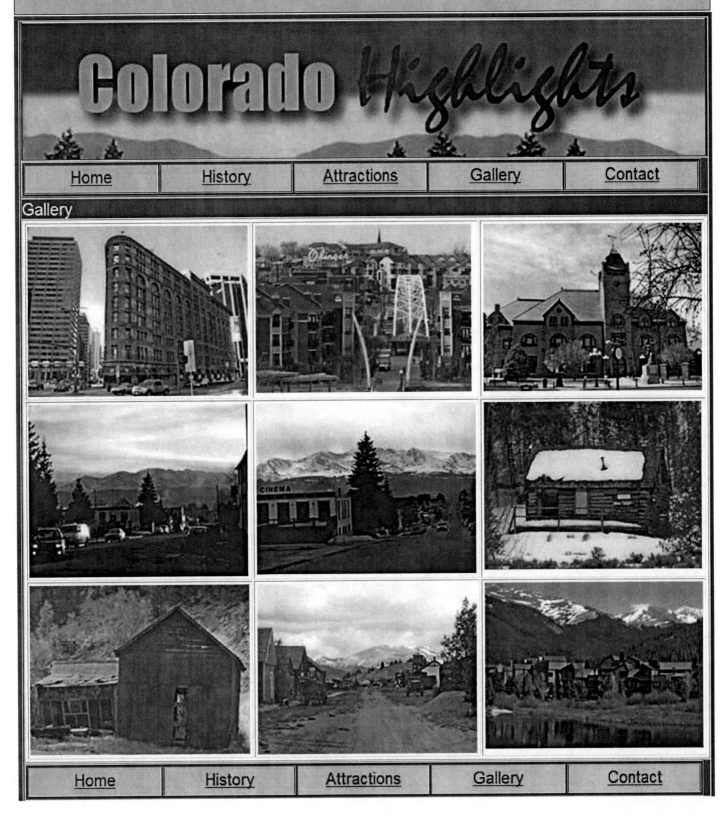

Activity 21: Microsoft Templates. These activities will allow you to download templates from the Microsoft website as long as you have legally purchased Microsoft Office. The number and quality of templates are plenty. It is definitely worth exploring. It can save time on design. If using Publisher or PowerPoint, you don't have to get templates online because it comes with so many built in designs.

Examples: The following is a list of several possible template formats that can be downloaded. By clicking on the **More categories**, you can see a lot more.

Some of the Microsoft templates include the following: agendas, awards certificates, brochures, budgets, business cards, calendars, content slides, contracts, databases, design slides, envelopes, flyers, gift certificates, invitations, job descriptions, letters, memos, newsletters, presentations, stationary, address books, advertisements, announcements, applications, banners, bookmarks, books, catalogs, charts, coloring and activity pages, coupons, flash cards, games, instructions, itineraries, journals, maps, math and science tables, menus, name and place cards, note cards, paper folding projects, photo albums, postcards, posters, quizzes and tests, quotes, recipes, signs, SmartArt Graphics, tickets, web pages, and more.

Some ideas for classroom projects: The templates are worth exploring. For example, if you were to click on the Book templates, you could find some of the following downloadable templates: a cookbook, a TV or movie script, a book manuscript, an autograph book, grade books, coloring books and more. There is even a student yearbook for junior high and high school. The journal templates have some great downloads with the following themes: My Camp Journal, Food diary, word journal, nutrition journal, and several other types of journals and diaries. There are several map downloads available as well. Some of the posters are worth exploring. The Science Fair Posters are very attractive and inviting. Students could download such templates and customize if for their school fair or other activity. The quizzes and tests have a lot of potential, the only dilemma is you need PowerPoint and Word 2007 to download many of these templates. When looking at the Photo Album templates, it became apparent that teachers could have their students use these templates for a variety of writing projects. They could incorporate their own photos and provide content to compliment the images. They could take a virtual trip around the world and put together a travel album. They could use their own photos and put together a digital representation with one of these templates.

Flyer Templates: Flyer templates can be used for thematic classroom projects. The following is an example of a flyer for ghost town tours in Colorado. You can get two different templates titled **flyer template** and **flyer template 2** in the **microsoft templates folder.** You can always go online and get premade templates on the Microsoft site. It should be helpful to see the examples that demonstrate how the final flyer might look for each template. Those are titled **flyer example** and **flyer example 2** in the same folder. See examples below!

COLO
GHOS
TOUI

Date: A

Time: 8:

Locatic

Denver, (

Every August, w
annual tour of C
famous ghost to
start our tour at
Colorado Histori
St. Elmo, Garfie
Vicksburg are ju
the towns we wi
a camera, curios
appetite.

SPONSORED BY C(

Colorado Ghost Town Tours

Every August, we take our annual tour of Colorado's famous ghost towns. We will start our tour at the Colorado Historical Society. St. Elmo, Garfield and Vicksburg are just a few of the towns we will visit. Bring a camera, curiosity and appetite.

Date: August 13th, 2010
Time: 8:00 a.m.
Location: 1300 Broadway, Denver Colorado 80203

Sponsored by Colorado Travel 303-333-3333

Brochure Templates: You can find the **PDF, brochures using Word 2007,** in the **Microsoft template** folder. This lesson shows how to make brochures in Microsoft 2007. You can view how to make brochures using Microsoft Word 2003: **Youtube:** http://www.youtube.com/watch?v=Uk07DVBXQ64

1. To get a thorough understanding of making brochures using Microsoft templates, watch my Youtube video: http://www.youtube.com/watch?v=Uk07DVBXQ64
2. Google Microsoft Templates. It should be the first site: http://office.microsoft.com/en-us/templates/default.aspx
3. Scroll down until you find the brochure templates.

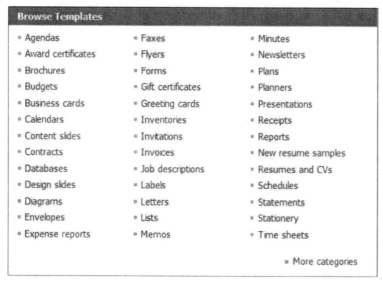

4. When the brochure template window pops up, scroll through until you find one that suites you needs. Be sure to pay attention to the version of Word or Publisher. Since this lesson will be demonstrated in Microsoft Word 2007, a template for Word 2007 or older can be downloaded.

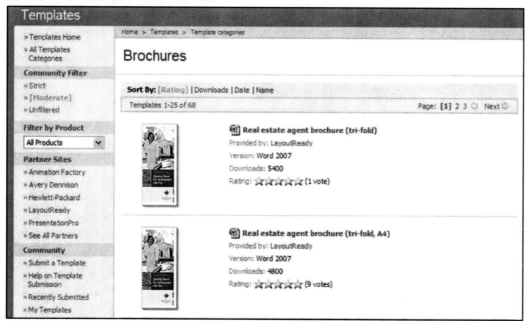

97

Travel Colorado

Tourist continue to come back to Colorado to view the majestic Mountains, see wildlife, visit inspiring museums, eat at affordable and tasty restaurants, ski some of the finest resorts, wander through the historical towns and imagine living in this special and fantastic state. This brochure will just give you a small sample of what is in store for you if you visit this great state.

Bison near Hartsel Colorado between Salida and Colorado Springs

Did you know that Colorado has the world's largest flat top mountain in Grand Mesa?

Denver: Denver, the capital city of Colorado, has a lot of wonderful amenities to offer tourists. Some of the museums include the Children's Museum, Museum of Contemporary Art, the Colorado History Museum and the Denver Art Museum. Another favorite spot in Denver is the 16th street mall. Denver offers free shuttle service for over a mile of shopping, eating and entertainment opportunities. Some other Denver attractions include the Denver Performing Arts, Coors Field, The Pepsi Center and the Colorado Convention Center

555 Downtown
Denver, CO 80202
Phone: 303-555-5555
travelcolo@gmail.com

History: Colorado has many historical spots. Mining played a major role in the history of Colorado. You can see remnants of mining activity in various locations throughout the Colorado Mountains. Colorado is also known for ghost towns. South Park, located in Fairplay, is a living history museum. It features over 34 historic buildings. Most of the buildings were moved into South Park from nearby communities.

Travel Colorado

Travel Colorado

This brochure will give you many reasons to travel to Colorado for your next vacation. It has beautiful scenery, ghost towns, cities, ski resorts, amusement parks, museums and more.

The Colorado Renaissance Festival: This unique and exciting festival takes place every summer. There is lively entertainment, historical shopping, unique characters and tasty eating.

Colorado Scenery: Colorado has 54 mountain peaks over 14,000 feet. There are over 630 peaks that reach 13,000 feet or higher. There are 25 scenic and historic byways in Colorado.

> **Newsletter:** You can find the **PDF, newsletter 2007**, in the **Microsoft template** folder. This lesson shows how to make newsletters in Microsoft 2007. This hand-out gives a great introduction for getting started in Publisher 2007.

1. Prior to creating any publications using Publisher, you should have the images saved in a safe and logical location on your computer.

2. To open Publisher, go to **Start | All Programs | Microsoft Office | Microsoft Office Publisher 2007**.

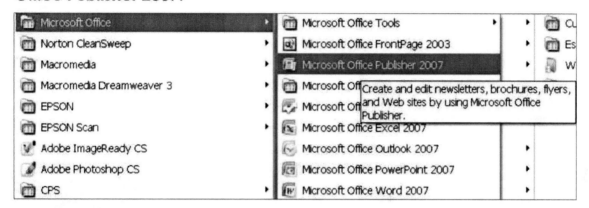

3. The following window should pop up:

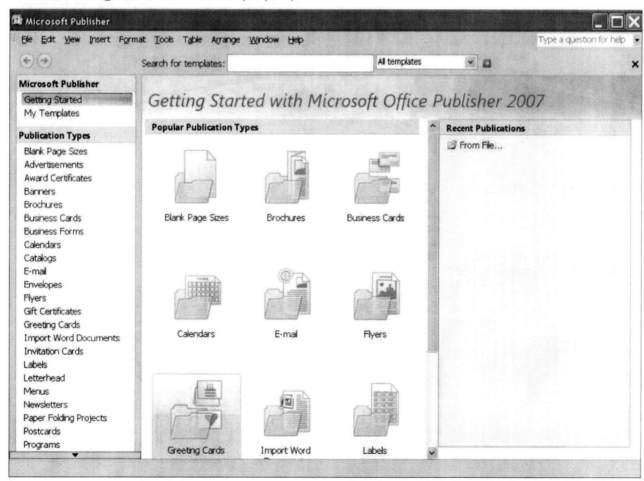

Colorado News

Volume 1, Issue 1   October 25, 2010

Colorado Travel

This newsletter is sold to over a million people a year throughout the nation. It keeps you updated on what really matters in this beautiful state.

Colorado Quick Facts

- Mt. Elbert is the tallest Mountain in Colorado, reaching a height of 14,433 feet.

- Grand Mesa is the world's largest flat top mountain.

- Leadville is the highest incorporated city in the United States at 10,430 feet elevation.

Colorado Renaissance Festival

The Colorado Renaissance takes place in Larkspur, CO on weekends throughout the summer. When you visit this festival, you feel like you have gone back in time with all the authentic costumes, smells and sounds. There are over 100 skilled artisans' exhibits. You can see many artisans create original works of art using techniques from the past.

You can witness the glass blower making unique and beautiful ware. You can observe how one artist can make Raku, pottery made using fire from a technique mastered in Japan during the 16th century. There are blacksmiths, wood workers, jewelry makers, leather making and more. In addition to viewing such marvelous creations, you can be entertained with music, comedy and other wonderful entertainment. An all time favorite is the fire eater. He is very entertaining and humorous. Don't forget to throw tomatoes at the tomato guy. He manages to insult just about anyone in his attempt to lure participants to pay money to throw tomatoes at his face. If you are easily

offended, you might avoid this guy. You can observe a procession of well costumed characters as they meander through the fair. In addition to all the wonderful entertainment, you can eat some roasted turkey legs, roasted corn, sausage or steak on a stick and some fresh baked goods. It is a great place to take family and friends. Don't miss the jousting!

Mining Towns

The rush to Colorado for gold took place in 1859 after prospectors discovered gold in vein deposits near present day Blackhawk and Central City. Since 1859, Colorado's mines have produced roughly 45 million ounces of gold. The largest discovery of gold was in the Cripple Creek district. Gold prospectors kept finding an unknown dark mineral instead of gold. It later became recognized as silver ore and lead. In 1879, molybdenum was discovered in Climax just north of Leadville. It had no known value until World War I when they realized it could be used to harden steel for armaments. Coal mining began soon after some of the first miners and settlers started arriving into the Front Range. Coal is still produced in the northwest part of the state.

Activity 22: Microsoft Excel can be a wonderful tool. Classrooms tend to use it for graphing activities and calculating data. The following activities might be considered non traditional uses of Excel. They are intended to be creative and interesting. The first activity can be used for a variety of topics. In this case it focuses on attractions around the world.

Attractions Around the World: The following is an example of part of the handout that students can use to complete an interactive activity on attractions around the world. To pick up this handout, visit the **Excel folder**. The title of the handout is **funplaces**.

Possible fun places: Check out the Examples PDF for ideas.

1. Copy **funplaces.xls** and paste it in a safe place on your computer.
2. Open it once it is in your folder.
3. Problem one is done as an example to demonstrate expectations.
4. Complete the **plan_funplaces** document.
5. Locate and save square shaped images of all the attractions on your **plan_funplaces** document. (see step 6)
6. The image should be shaped like a square, since the image placed in the project is shaped like a square. If you get rectangular shapes, the image will lose quality. You can always use an image editing program to make the image a square.
7. Once you saved your images on your computer, you can insert them in the square autoshape of the **funplaces.xls** spreadsheet.
8. To insert images, right click on the square **autoshape**. For 2003, choose the **Format AutoShape** option from the drop down menu. When the **Format AutoShape** window pops up, select the **Colors and Lines** tab. Under the **Fill** section, choose **Fill Effects**. After selecting **Fill Effects**, click on the **Picture** tab. For 2007, choose **Picture** after clicking on the drop down menu of the paint bucket.

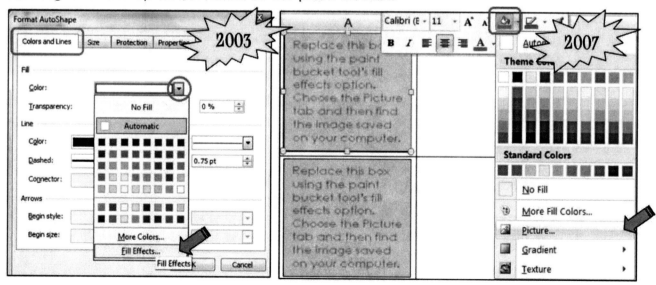

9. After selecting Picture in either 2003 or 2007, an **Insert Picture** window will pop up.

Cool Places for Kids to Travel

Directions: Choose at least 10 places to represent in your interactive activity in Microsoft Excel. You are welcome to use fun places that aren't on the list. Use places that most students have never heard of.

- Alcatraz
- Angel Falls
- Angkor Wat
- Arches National park
- The Badlands
- Barringer Meteor Crater
- Blue Holes of Andros
- The Blue Mosque
- Bora Bora
- Bran Castle/Dracula's Castle
- Brooklyn Bridge
- Bryce Canyon
- Cappadocia
- Carlsbad Caverns
- Catacombs of Rome
- Cliffs of Moher
- Colosseum
- Crater Lake
- Crystal River
- The Dead Sea
- Death Valley
- Easter Island
- The Eiffel Tower
- Empire State Building
- Ephesus
- The Everglades
- Fez Medina
- Florissant Fossil Beds
- The Forbidden City
- Galapagos
- The Giant's Causeway
- Golden Gate Bridge

- Jericho
- The Kremlin
- Kruger National Park
- Lake Baikal
- Lake Titicaca
- Leaning Tower of Pisa
- Machu Picchu
- Maelstrom
- Mammoth Cave
- Meenakshi Temple
- Mesa Verde
- Mauna Loa
- Monument Valley
- Mount Fuji
- Mount Rushmore
- Museo de las Momias
- The Nazca Lines
- Neuschwanstein Castle
- Newgrange
- Niagara Falls
- Pamukkale
- Petra
- Petrified Forest
- Phang Nga Bay
- Pitch Lake
- Pompeii
- The Pompidou Center
- Potala Palace
- The Ross Ice Shelf
- Rotorua
- Salar de Uyuni
- Sargasso Sea

Plan: The following handout provides students a plan prior to setting up their project in Excel. This handout, **plan_funplaces**, can be found in the **Excel folder.** If the attraction being represented in this assignment can have more than one name, the student needs to list all the possible names in the last column. This assignment can easily be customized for a variety of topics, including famous or infamous people, U.S. presidents, World Geography, inventions, landmarks, etc.

Planning for your interactive activity in Excel

Directions: Choose 10 or more places you want to represent in your Excel project. Type it under the **Place/Answer** column. Type the clues under the **Clue** column. The clue shouldn't give too much information, but enough to help the user find the information by doing an efficient key word search. If there is more than one possible answer, type in all the possible answers under the **If an Or statement** column. The first two are examples of how this document should be set up.

#	Place/Answer	Clues for your place of interest (complete sentences with no grammatical errors)	If an OR statement, type in all the possible answers
1	Mesilla	The famous trial of Billy the Kid was held in this town. The Plaza in this town was listed on the National Register in January 1982.	
2	Great Sand Dunes	This park is home to the tallest dunes in North America.	Great Sand Dunes National Park, Great Sand Dunes, Great Sand Dunes National Park and Preserve
3			
4			
5			
6			
7			
8			
9			
10			
11			
12			

Template: The following template will be modified by students. This spreadsheet, **funplaces,** can be found in the **Excel folder.** The first one in the spreadsheet is an example so students can see how the interactive spreadsheet can be set up. This template can be used in a variety of projects. You can change it from Fun Places to Great Inventions or Inventors, Famous or Infamous Leaders, Artists from Around the World, States, Countries, etc. To add images under Fun Places, watch the **auto-shape tips** video in the **video folder.**

Fun Places for Kids to Travel

Directions: Set up each problem like the example shown below. It will be set up so that when a user scrolls over the Answer column, a clue is provided. When they type in the answer and press on the enter key of the keyboard, feedback will be provided under the Feedback section. The clues shouldn't give too much information but enough to find the answer if the user performs an efficient

Fun Places	Answers	Feedback
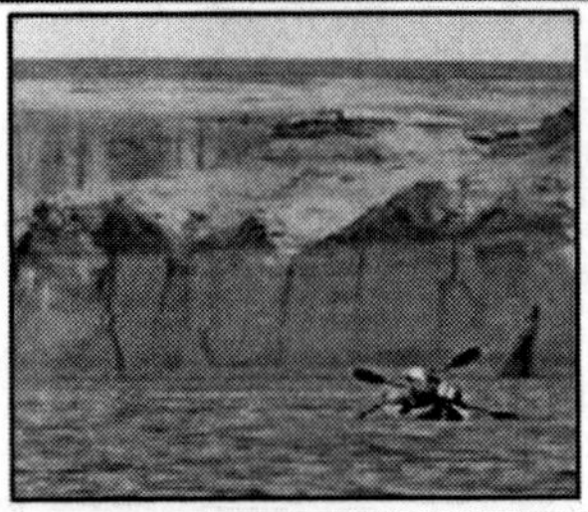	Lake Powell	Great Job!
Replace this box using the paint bucket tool's fill effects option. Choose the Picture tab and then find the image saved on your		
Replace this box using the paint bucket tool's fill effects option. Choose the Picture tab and then find the image saved on your		
Replace this box using the paint bucket tool's fill effects option. Choose the Picture tab and then find the image saved on your		

Students have a great time setting up this interactive game. If you find any flaws, feel free to contact me at kidsnetsoft@gmail.com

Rubric: The rubric can be located in the **Excel folder**. It should help guide students through this lesson so they can create a meaningful and interactive product. This rubric can easily be transferred to projects related to other thematic units.

Accuracy of Content	All information in the hints category is accurate.	All but one fact in the information in the hints category is accurate.	At least two facts in the information of the hints category are accurate.	Several statements in the hints category are inaccurate.
Attractiveness	All images used to represent the clues are of good quality and of the same size.	All but one image used to represent the clues is of good quality and of the same size.	At least two images used to represent the clues are of poor quality and of the same size.	Several images used to represent the clues are of poor quality and of the same size.
Clues	The clues given distinguish the answer from other possible answers without immediately giving the answer away.	Most of the clues given distinguish the answer from other possible answers without immediately giving the answer away.	Some of the clues given distinguish the answer from other possible answers without immediately giving the answer away.	Few if any clues given distinguish the answer from other possible answers without immediately giving the answer away.
Spelling and Grammar	No spelling and grammar errors were made.	At least one spelling and grammar error was made.	Some spelling and grammar errors were made.	Several spelling and grammar errors were made.
Feedback	All feedback is appropriate and accurate. There are more than 5 different responses in the feedback section. Two or more feedbacks include the OR function.	All feedback is appropriate and accurate. There are less than 5 and more than two different responses in the feedback section. Less than two feedbacks include the OR function.	All feedback is appropriate and accurate. There are only two different responses in the feedback section. None of the feedbacks involve the OR function.	Most feedback is appropriate and accurate. There are only two different responses in the feedback section. None of the feedbacks involve the OR function.

Directions: Once you have evaluated your own project, provide feedback to your peers so they can make changes based on your feedback. Evaluate at least one or more people. Thoroughly evaluate their project so they can make meaningful changes to their product. You may or may not be graded on the accuracy of your feedback. For instance, if you give the person you are evaluating a 10 on spelling and grammar and there are mistakes in this area, you may lose points. Your meaningful feedback is important in this lesson.

Rate students from 0-10, with 10 being the highest

Category	9-10	6-8	3-5	0-2	Feedback given to person being evaluated
Accuracy of Content					
Attractiveness					
Clues					
Spelling and Grammar					
Feedback					

Activity 23: PowerPoint Quote's Unit: Students pick a theme for this quotes unit. They find quotes and visually represent them in a PowerPoint presentation. In addition to getting powerful quotes, students get to learn about design. The first handout students will need is the **plan quotes** document in the **quotes unit folder.** The following is an example of how the document could look when complete. This document is titled **plan quotes example.**

Directions: Find 10 or more quotes to put into a PowerPoint presentation. Each quote will have a large image to compliment its message. If it is an unknown author, type in anonymous. You can choose from quotes available on the following link: http://www.kidsnetsoft.com/html/quotes.html or use quotes provided below the table. Some students have chosen themes such as funny quotes or random quotes. The quotes below are powerful and meaningful.

#	Quote (be sure to put exact words in quotes)	Author's Name
1	"We have forgotten how to be good guests, how to walk lightly on the earth as its other creatures do."	Barbara Ward
2	"It feels so good not to be a slave to gas, playing the whole game of war for oil."	~Daryl Hannah
3	"My lens of choice was always the 35 mm. It was more environmental. You can't come in closer with the 35 mm."	~Annie Leibovitz
4	"Adopt the pace of nature: her secret is patience."	~Author Unknown
5	"For 200 years we've been conquering Nature. Now we're beating it to death."	~Tom McMillan
6	"Take care of the earth and she will take care of you."	~Author Unknown
7	"The activist is not the man who says the river is dirty. The activist is the man who cleans up the river."	~Ross Perot
8	"Take nothing but pictures. Leave nothing but footprints. Kill nothing but time."	~Motto of the Baltimore Grotto
9	"Every day should be Earth Day."	~Author Unknown
10	"Man is a complex being: he makes deserts bloom - and lakes die."	~Gil Stern

1. "Reading is to the mind what exercise is to the body." -- Joseph Addison
2. "If you have much, give your wealth. If you have little, give your heart." -- Arab proverb

Directions: Follow all the steps to create a powerful presentation about famous quotes.

1. Create a folder named **Quotes** in a safe location on your computer.
2. Pick up and complete the **plan quotes** document before creating your presentation.
3. Open Microsoft PowerPoint by choosing **Start | All Programs | Microsoft Office | PowerPoint**
4. If the **Slide Layout** window isn't showing, choose **Format | Slide Layout** from the main menu

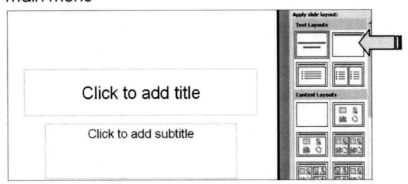

5. Choose the **Title** layout, since you will only need an image and a text box.
6. Save your presentation because it is the smart thing to do by choosing **File | Save as** from the main menu.
7. Locate your **Quotes folder** and name the presentation **quotes**.
8. Find a large image online for your introduction page. **Right click** and choose **Copy** from the drop down menu.

9. Return to your PowerPoint and choose **Edit | Paste** or use the shortcut **Ctrl + V**. Center your image on the page. Add your title in the text box. If the text box isn't showing, it is likely that it is hidden under the image. To get the text box on top, right click on the image and choose **Order | Send to Back**. The text box should appear. If the text box still isn't showing, choose **Insert | Text** from the main menu. Click on the slide and type in your title.

Examples: The following is an example of the handout to apply transitions, custom animations and timings for the PowerPoint presentation. You can pick up the handout **transitions** in the **quotes unit folder.** This handout will come in handy for the next activity on Book Presentations.

1. When all your slides are complete, you can add transitions and custom animations.
2. Personally, I don't even bother with custom animations. I just add a simple transition for every slide.
3. To add a transition, click on your first slide.
4. Choose **Slide Show | Slide Transition** from the main menu.
5. A window should pop up with your transition options.

Great Tips: When you click on the transition, it will demonstrate immediately what that transition will look like. You can make a selection; change the speed in the **Speed** section. You can also apply a sound when that transition occurs. Personally, unless it is necessary for the presentation, this option should b e avoided. This particular presentation will have a song playing throughout the duration of the slide show, so any sound would be distracting. Since consistency is considered a critical part of design, you should choose the **Apply to All Slides** once you have chosen the slide and speed of the transition. Avoid too many distractions by keeping your presentation consistent. An audience shouldn't have to be focusing on the "cool" transitions you continuously change for every slide.

6. Once you have applied your transitions, if you think it is really essential to add Custom Animations, click on the first slide and choose **Slide Show | Custom Animations** from the main menu.

Examples: The following is an example of the handout for adding sound throughout the duration of your PowerPoint presentation. You can pick up the handout **sound** in the **quotes unit folder.** This handout will come in handy for the next activity on Book Presentations.

1. In the transitions handout, the directions warned to keep track of the seconds in the timings so that you could get sound to last the duration of the presentation.
2. Once you have the seconds of the presentation, add approximately 10 more seconds because the music might end before the presentation.
3. Open a sound editing program if you have such access. In this case, Audacity will be used.
4. Open Audacity by choosing the Start menu. Choose **All Programs | Audacity.**
5. Open a song by choosing File | Open from the main menu.
6. If you get an error message or the sound isn't working properly once opened in Audacity, you might need to convert the sound to a different format. If you can't convert the sound and open it in Audacity, you can play the music on your computer and record it into Audacity. Be sure to set it to Stereo Mix.

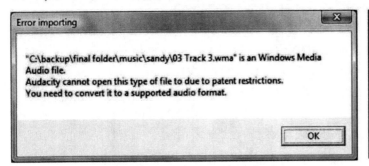

Audacity supports .wavs and .mp3s. There is conversion software available.

7. With your song open in Audacity, clip out the sound you don't need. According to my timings, the presentation was 42 seconds. I will then clip out after 52 seconds to give a little extra music.
8. Select what you want to delete and then click on the delete key of your keyboard.

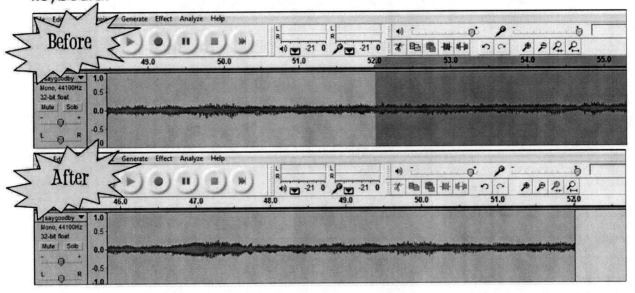

Examples: The following are some examples of what the slides look like. Take note of the consistency of layout, color scheme, font choices, image and quote location. The presentation can be viewed as a demonstration. It is located in the **quotes folder** that is nested in the **quotes unit folder.**

Quotes by Chris Clementi

Image source: Darrell Vanaman

"We have forgotten how to be good guests, how to walk lightly on the earth as its other creatures do." By Barbara Ward

Image source: Chris Clementi

"Every day should be Earth Day." by ~ author unknown

Image source: Chris Clementi

"Man is a complex being: he makes deserts bloom - and lakes die." by ~Gil Stern

Image source: Darrell Vanaman

"It feels so good not to be a slave to gas, playing the whole game of war for oil." by ~Daryl Hannah

Image source: Darrell Vanaman

"Adopt the pace of nature: her secret is patience." by ~ Author unknown

Rubric: The following is an example of page one of the rubric. It is a word document so that you can customize it according to your specifications in your class. It is titled **quotes rubric** and it can be located in the **quotes unit folder**.

Presentation	Well-rehearsed with smooth delivery that holds audience attention.	Rehearsed with fairly smooth delivery that holds audience attention most of the time.	Delivery not smooth, but able to maintain interest of the audience most of the time.	Delivery not smooth and audience attention often lost.
Music	Music compliments the quotes stirring emotions from the audience. The music fades in and fades out. It lasts the entire duration of the presentation.	Music compliments the quotes stirring emotions from the audience. The music fades in and fades out. The music doesn't last the entire duration of the presentation.	Music compliments the quotes somewhat stirring emotions from the audience. The music doesn't fade in and out. The music doesn't last the entire duration of the presentation.	Music doesn't compliment the quotes. The music doesn't fade in and out. The music doesn't last the entire duration of the presentation.
Work Ethic	Student always uses classroom project time well. Conversations are primarily focused on the project and things needed to get the work done and are held in a manner that typically does not disrupt others.	Student usually uses classroom project time well. Most conversations are focused on the project and things needed to get the work done and are held in a manner that typically does not disrupt others.	Student usually uses classroom project time well, but occasionally distracts others from their work.	Student does not use classroom project time well OR typically is disruptive to the work of others.
Grammar & Spelling (Conventions)	Writer makes no errors in grammar or spelling that distracts the reader from the content.	Writer makes 1-2 errors in grammar or spelling that distract the reader from the content.	Writer makes 3-4 errors in grammar or spelling that distract the reader from the content.	Writer makes more than 4 errors in grammar or spelling that distract the reader from the content.

Activity 24: PowerPoint Book Presentation: Students record their favorite sentence from all the chapters of a book they are reading. Once they come up with their favorite sentence, they will visually represent it in a PowerPoint presentation. This same concept could be transferred to other multi-media platforms. However, in this example, the presentation will be in PowerPoint. Students need a handout and a template for this activity. The handout, titled **plan presentation** can be found in the **book presentation folder** along with the **PowerPoint template** to create the project.

Planning Book Presentation

Directions: For each chapter, write down your favorite sentence and then find an image to visually represent that sentence. Once you locate a large quality image, shaped like a square, save it in a folder somewhere safe on your computer. (If you know how to crop images, you don't have to get square shaped images) Be sure to write the image source under the correct column. Don't put the entire website address. For instance, if the website is http://www.nytimes.com/ type in **nytimes** under **Image Source**. If you need to add more chapters, click in the last row, last column and click on the Tab key of your keyboard.

#	Chapter Name	Favorite Sentence from the Chapter.	Image source
1			
2			
3			
4			
5			
6			
7			
8			
9			
10			
11			
12			
13			
14			
15			
16			
17			
18			
19			
20			
21			

Don't forget to watch the autoshape tips video if you haven't already.

Directions: Follow each step to create a multimedia presentation using Microsoft PowerPoint. Whatever you do, do not change the font until the presentation is complete.

1. **Copy** the PowerPoint called **powerpoint_template** and the document titled **plan presentation** from a location specified by your teacher.
2. Once they are pasted in a safe location on your computer, you can **open** them. You can complete the plan presentation before you create your PowerPoint presentation.
3. The presentation is set up for 5 chapters. To add more chapters, click on the last slide and choose **Insert | Duplicate Slide** (Word 2003) or choose the **Home** tab and click on the drop down arrow of **New Slide** and pick **Duplicate Selected Slides.** (Word 2007) This will allow you to maintain consistency for all your main slides. Consistency is important for good design.

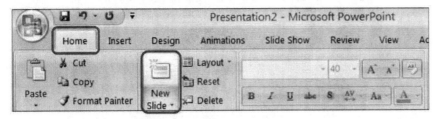

4. Replace the **text box** with your **favorite sentence** from the chapter being represented. Be sure to put the sentence in **quotes** to avoid plagiarism.
5. Find an **image** to compliment each sentence from all the chapters.
6. When getting images, get larger images shaped more like a square, since the shape of the image is like a square. If you get images that aren't shaped like a square, the end results will be distorted.
7. When you find an appropriate image online, **Right click** on the image and choose **Save Picture As.**

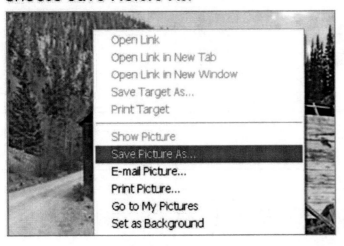

If you know how to crop images, you don't have to be limited to images shaped like squares. The following steps will demonstrate the difference between image shapes and their final outcome.

Activity 25: Microsoft Moviemaker. You can pick up the user friendly handout called **moviemaker.pdf** in the **moviemaker folder.**

Directions: These directions could be for any project. The examples for this assignment are meant for a student's interpretation of problems the world faces today. The example in this demonstration will have sound, transitions, images and video.

1. Create a folder somewhere safe on your computer and name it **moviemaker.**
2. Place at least 10-15 (number will vary depending on the length of your presentation) images in the moviemaker folder. The images should be roughly the same size to maintain quality and prevent distortion. If you plan on expanding your movie to take up the entire size of your monitor, you will want large images.
3. If getting images online, be sure to only look for large images. If doing a Google search, you can click on **Show options**. You can record on a word document what source you used to get your images. Don't bother putting the entire website address. For example, if it is http://www.nationalgeographic.com/ you can type National Geographic to credit the image source at the end of the presentation.

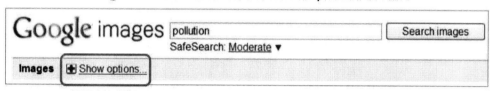

4. Once **Show options** is selected, click on **Large**.

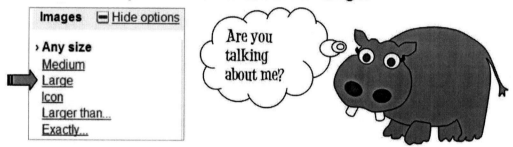

5. If you don't plan on cropping your images, you need to only get images shaped like a landscape versus a portrait, since the final movie is shaped like a landscape. Examples A and C would work for the presentation, while examples B and D would result in poor results. See step 6 for a better example.

115

Title of project is "Problems in the 21st Century"

#	Image name	Source
1	Poverty1	solarnavigator
2	Poverty2	oikocredit
3	Poverty3	British Helsinki Human Rights Gro...
4	Poverty4	Photography Blog
5	Pollution1	CUNY
6	Pollution2	Lesradins
7	Pollution3	Waste...
8	Pollution4	Digg
9	Deforest1	Jay Pitocch...
10	Deforest2	Rhett Butler
11	Deforest3	Pacific ...
12	Deforest4	Gallerie D'Imma...
13	Endangered1	Galaxy Photo
14	Endangered2	First People
15	Endangered3	China Giant Panda
16	Endangered4	Marine Conservation
17	Endangered5	Worth 1000
18	War1	War Photo
19	War2	Ruins of a Civil War
20	War3	Iraqi Children
21	War4	PPOOPP
22	War5	Martin Goodman
23	War6	Children and War
24	Crime1	Layne Kennedy
25	Crime2	Tom G. Palmer
26	Crime3	Marco Razpet
27	Crime4	Wylie, Texas Police
28	Overpopulation1	Teaching Montessori
29	Overpopulation2	Functional Ambivalent
30	Overpopulation3	Wangjianshuo's Blog
31	Overpopulation4	Trek Earth
32	Desertification1	Arcadis
33	Desertification2	Remi Benali

Youtube
Kidsnetsoft
to see the World
Problems example

Examples: Students can pick up a word document titled **history** in the **moviemaker folder.** They can keep track of their image, sound and video sources so they can properly credit them at the end of the presentation. An example is provided so students can see what this document might look like when completed. This PDF, called **history_example** can be picked up in the **moviemaker folder.**

Directions: You will be picking 1-2 events from each year ranging in a 10 year timeframe. You will have at least 5 different video clips of no more than 10 seconds and at least 10 quality images to compliment the time periods.

What time frame are you covering? 1900-1909

Year	Event	Audio/video/image source
1900	Boxer Rebellion	Pri egon
1901	U.S. President McKinley was assassina	
1902	Mount Pelée Erupts	
1903	First Silent Movie	
1903	First World Series	
1904	Ground Broken on Panama Canal	ar
1904	New York City Subway Opens	Stu math
1904	Russo-Japanese War Begins	Ww A/video
1905	Russian Revolution	Levan Ramishvili
1905	Einstein Proposes His Theory of Relativity	IACvi
1906	Kellogg's Starts Selling Corn Flakes	Weenielongus
1906	San Francisco Earthquake	The Earth Quake Channel
1907	First Electric Washing Machine	Commons.wikimedia
1907	Picasso Introduces Cubism	Archive.com
1908	Ford Introduces the Model-T	experimenta69
1909	NAACP Is Founded	naacpvideos

Youtube
Kidsnetsoft
to see the World
History example

Examples: Students can pick up a word document titled **Promoting a Charity** in the **moviemaker folder.** They can keep track of their image, sound and video sources so they can properly credit them at the end of the presentation. An example is provided so students can see what this document might look like when completed. This PDF, called **Promoting a Charity Example** can be picked up in the **moviemaker folder.** In addition to charities, this same document could be used to promote a cause like water conservation, anti pollution, alternative fuel, etc.

Directions: Chose a worthy and reliable cause to promote. Once you have determined which organization you want to advertise, fill in the table below to assist in your organization to create a Movie or other multi-media presentation. To stay organized, name the object (image or video) as object1, object2, etc. so that you can easily place them on the timeline in Movie Maker or whatever application you choose to use.

Script	Photo or video description	object	video
UNICEF is a child advocacy organization that works for over 150 countries.	Video of UNICEF helping children		
They have highly skilled staff members that consist of public health, disease prevention, human rights, and education.	Video of doctors helping poor nations.	obj	Doctors without Borders Video
UNICEF's goal is to provide children with clean water, health care, nutrition, education, emergency relief and more.	Image of child drinking water.	object3	Wordpress
Did you know that roughly 2 million people, mostly children, die from unsafe water?	Child drinking unsafe water	object4	MrMurphys73
UNICEF works in more than 90 countries to promote sanitary access to water and safe hygiene practices.	Teaching about sanitary and hygienic practices	object5	UNICEF Video

Youtube Kidsnetsoft to see the Promoting Charity example

Storyboarding

Directions: Come up with a plan to create a multimedia presentation. You can either draw or write keywords of the image/video you will have for each idea. Write a brief script to assist in the organization and production of your movie.

Storyboarding

Directions: Come up with a plan to create a multimedia presentation. You can either draw, write keywords of the image/video or insert an image for each idea or script. Write a brief script or dialogue to assist in the organization and production of your movie. Each rounded rectangular **AutoShape** can be replaced with images by using the paint bucket tool or you can use digital drawing tools to draw a rough draft of the scene. The first three scenes have been done as an example.

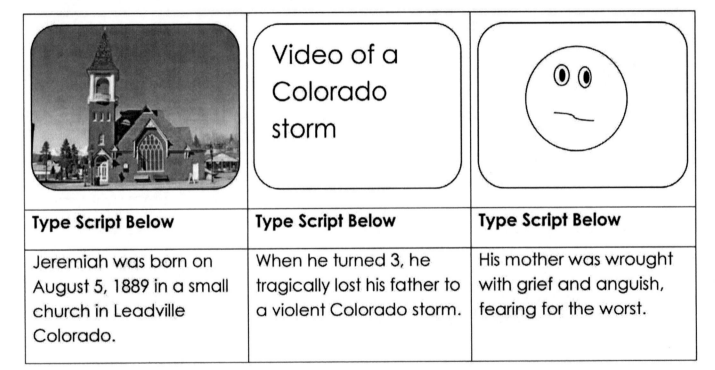

Type Script Below	Type Script Below	Type Script Below
Jeremiah was born on August 5, 1889 in a small church in Leadville Colorado.	When he turned 3, he tragically lost his father to a violent Colorado storm.	His mother was wrought with grief and anguish, fearing for the worst.

If you want to have students pick up the storyboard on the computer instead of printing storyboard1 or storyboard2, have them digitally pick up storyboard3. They can draw or write what the image/video will be in the proper column and then write the script.

Activity 26 Google Applications: This unit will focus on many of the wonderful tools available with Google in Education. You will get fabulous ideas that will allow you to collaborate with teachers and students.

Google Templates: The following is an example of part of the handout to create Google Documents using templates. This assignment will give your staff and students the opportunity to create from a variety of templates. This lesson also demonstrates how to create and submit your own templates to the public for use. Pick up this handout titled **Google templates** in the **Google folder**.

1. Watch some of the videos to get a general overview of Google Docs Templates:

   - http://www.youtube.com/watch?v=G4ZnjAMMgkY&feature=PlayList&p=61 4459C76DAB68AC&playnext=1&playnext_from=PL&index=57

   - http://www.youtube.com/watch?v=u8BdW71Gcno

2. There are a couple of ways to access Google Docs Templates. You can click on **Documents** once you are logged into Google.

3. There is a **Search Templates** link that will allow you to access all the Google Docs Templates.

4. A page will open with a variety of template options. You can see the multitude of choices in the left hand column. You can even contribute by submitting your own template.

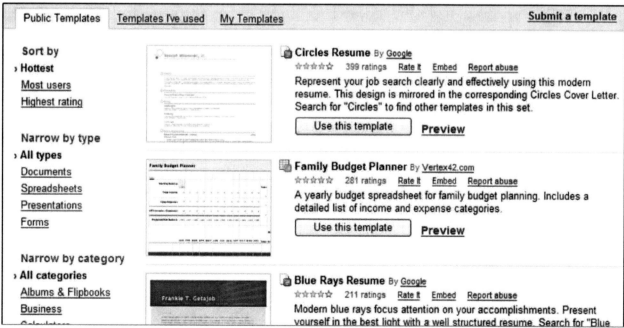

G-Mail The following is an example of part of the handout for using Gmail. This is a great start for preparing for some of the more elaborate units using Google for Education. The handout titled **Google Mail** can be found in the **Google folder.**

Directions: This document is intended to give you a breakdown of a variety of wonderful features that are part of Google's services for education.

Gmail

1. Set up a Gmail account if you haven't already: http://www.gmail.com

2. Managing your Gmail. Take note of the options in your Gmail window:

Gmail options: Inbox allows you to read your e-mails. The Starred option allows you to select the star next to an e-mail you might want to get to quickly later. If you star an email and then click on Starred, it will bring up all the e-mails that you starred earlier. You can view your sent mail and drafts. The next steps will talk about setting up contacts.

3. When clicking on **Contacts**, you have several options. You can set up friends, family, and coworkers. Notice the + sign and one person. That is for setting up one contact. When clicking on the **New Contact** for one person, a window with a variety of fields will pop up for you to enter an assortment of information. It isn't necessary to enter all the data. The Full name and e-mail will be fine.

4. When clicking on the **New Group**, you can set up your classroom.

5. Type in the new group's name when the window pops up after clicking on the **New Group** icon.

1. Watch the following YouTube videos on Google Apps to get a general idea about Google Forms:

   Basics on forms: http://www.youtube.com/watch?v=IzgaUOW6GIs
   Setting up a quiz: http://www.youtube.com/watch?v=xC1L0wpmqIY
   Contact forms: http://www.youtube.com/watch?v=YxYZKkusg-Y

2. Go to Google Forms for Education:
   http://docs.google.com/support/bin/answer.py?hl=en&answer=87809

3. Select **Google Docs** once you are logged into Google.

4. Choose **New | Form** from the menu.

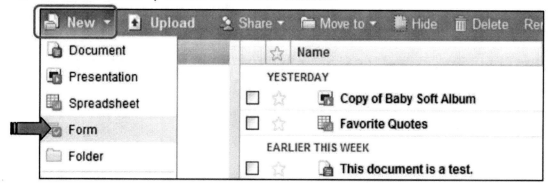

5. When the form pops up, you can start creating your questions. Type in the question in the **Question Title**. Add text in the **Help Text** section if the question might be vague. Choose the **Question Type**. In this example, it will be a **Multiple choice** question.

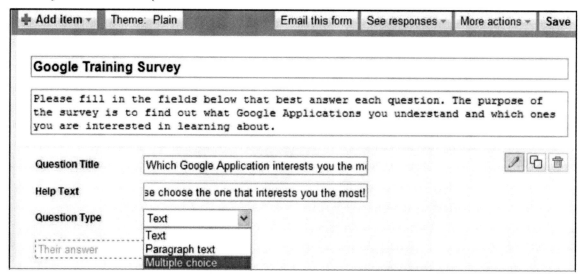

123

Example of a Form: The following is an example of what a form could look like. There are a variety of attractive templates to choose from. Some teachers have used it to gather information from their students, parents or colleagues. It can also be used to create quizzes like the one below.

Answer the following questions pertaining to South American Geography.

* Required

Mountains cover roughly 80% of this country. *

○ Peru

○ Chile

○ Argentina

○ Paraguay

○ Columbia

What major issue did Columbia and the U.S. collaborate on in the 1980s? This issue is still a huge problem in Columbia. *

Check off Paraguay's major exports. *

☐ Soybeans

☐ Feed

☐ Fish

☐ Cotton

☐ Meat

Submit

Google Docs: The following is an example of part of the handout to create Google Docs. This assignment will give your staff and students a great opportunity to collaborate with each other for a variety of purposes. Pick up this handout titled **Google Docs** in the **Google folder**.

1. Go to Google Apps Education Edition for an overview of all the classroom possibilities: http://www.google.com/educators/p_apps.html

2. Watch the following YouTube videos on Google Apps to get a general idea about its capabilities:

   - http://www.youtube.com/watch?v=kJT3pagjd8s&feature=channel

   - http://www.youtube.com/watch?v=TYPjJK6LZdM

   - http://www.youtube.com/watch?v=jVjwKmDLrlE&feature=PlayList&p=372A76 C86AF35D52&playnext=1&playnext_from=PL&index=6

3. If you are logged into your Google account, choose **Documents** from the menu. It will either be in the main menu or under **more**.

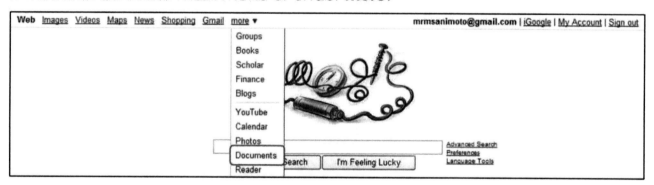

4. You can also go to http://docs.google.com/

5. Notice there are no documents in this account. That will change soon.

6. To create a Google Doc, click on the "**New** button to create a new online document." You can also click on the **Upload** button to edit a file saved on your computer.

Google Calendar

Directions: follow the steps to learn how to use Google calendar to stay organized.

1. Watch the following videos for an overview of Google calendar:

   - http://www.youtube.com/watch?v=2iTsxQFvQZQ

   - http://www.youtube.com/watch?v=1qsZUbVqUZc

2. Click on the Google **Calendar** link once you have logged into your Google Account.

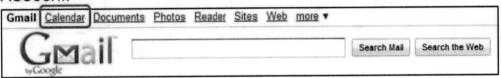

3. When the calendar loads, it might look like the following example.

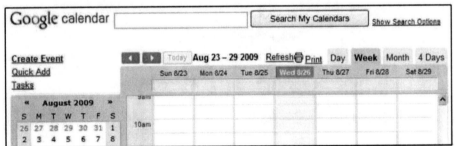

4. To create an event, click on the **Create Event** option or double click on the day you want to add an event. When the following window pops up, you can type in what the event will be and then click on the **Create event** button. You can also click on edit event details to add more detailed information and to invite people to view your calendar if necessary.

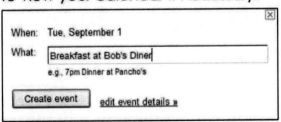

5. To edit the event, you can double click on the event on the calendar and make necessary changes.

Google Sites: The following is an example of part of the handout to create Google Sites. This assignment will give your staff and students the opportunity to create Google Sites. Pick up this handout titled **Google Sites** in the **Google folder**.

Directions: Google Sites allows you to create websites, using some of their built in themes. You can upload attachments, add links, insert images, post announcements or imbed documents. You can invite others to manage your site by giving them privileges. You can limit who can see your WebPages if necessary.

Helpful Videos:

- http://www.youtube.com/watch?v=fD-4FRTzxkl
- http://www.youtube.com/watch?v=X_KnC2EIS5w
- http://www.youtube.com/watch?v=X_KnC2EIS5w&feature=PlayList&p=43EA6 8CD3CDDF704&playnext=1&playnext_from=PL&index=38

Getting Started:

1. Go to Google: http://www.google.com/
2. If you don't have a G-mail account, sign up for one.
3. If Sites isn't in the main Google menu at the top, click on **Sites** under **more** options once you are logged in to your Google account. You can also type **sites.google.com/** in the URL.

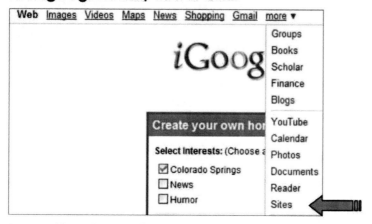

4. You will get a welcome window. When this pops up, click on the **Create Site** option.

Google Earth: The following is an example of part of the handout to use Google Earth. This assignment will give your staff and students the opportunity to do creative and interesting assignments using Google Earth. Pick up this handout titled **Google Earth** in the **Google folder.**

1. Download Google Earth 5.0 or higher: http://earth.google.com/

2. You might want to watch a couple of the videos for an overview of Google Earth.

   Google Earth Basics: http://www.youtube.com/watch?v=PAp0q_dLTmk
   Google Earth 5.0: http://www.youtube.com/watch?v=GSuJq4UzklA
   Ocean in 3D: http://www.youtube.com/watch?v=KOG-iAiDiko

3. Open up Google Earth and you should get a window that is similar to the following example. A tip window should pop up. It might be worth exploring.

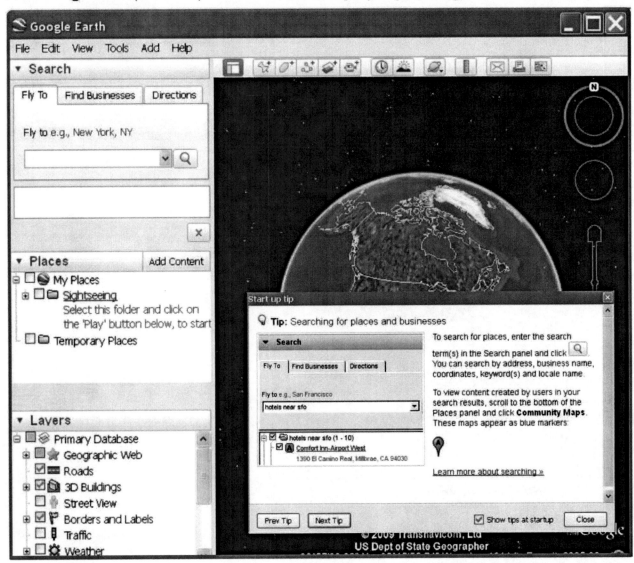

Google Maps: The following is an example of part of the handout to use Google Maps. This assignment will give your staff and students the opportunity to do creative and interesting assignments using Google Maps. Pick up this handout titled **Google Maps** in the **Google folder.**

1. Complete your Plan Your Map document.

2. Go to http://maps.google.com/

3. Watch the following videos: http://www.youtube.com/watch?v=ft7FZe6Q8OI ; http://www.youtube.com/watch?v=TftFnot5uXw

4. Sign in to Google Maps if you haven't already.

5. When logged in to Google Maps, if you click on the **Get Directions** link, you can type in where you want to go by typing in the address of the location you are starting and typing in the location of where you want to go. You can specify how you plan on travelling. You can get directions by car, public transit, or walking.

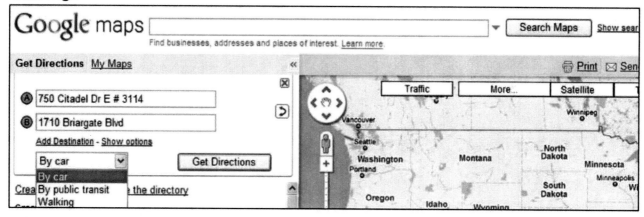

6. When clicking on **Get Directions** and travelling by car, the directions appeared in the left hand section of the window.

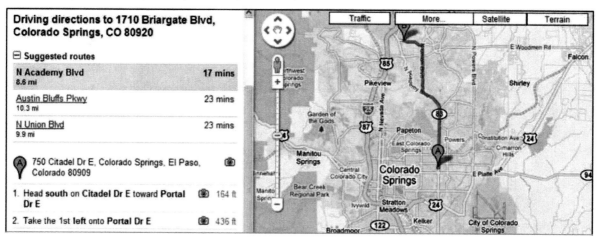

Google Maps: The following is an example of the plan for the map activity. You can pick up the template for this activity in the **Google Folder** titled **Plan Your Map.**

Directions: This document can be customized to whatever plan you have for your Google Map activity. Three or more facts should be added for each attraction. To add more rows, click in the last cell and last row of the table and click on the Tab key of your keyboard. This example is for a tour of Europe.

#	City, Country	Attraction	Information	Source
1	Rome, Italy	Colosseum	The Colosseum was established in 80 A.D. It was the first permanent amphitheatre to be built in Rome. It can seat 50,000 spectators. Wild animals would be brought into the Colosseum to fight gladiators.	Great Buildings
2	Vatican City	Vatican City	The Vatican City is its own country that lies within the city of Rome. Vatican city maintains diplomatic relations with over 150 countries. The Pope of this holy city ministers over a billion Roman Catholics. As of 2004, they had a population of 798 people.	National Geographic
3	Colditz Castle	Near Leipzig Germany	The Colditz Castle was originally built as a hunting lodge for the King of Saxony in 1014. It has been destroyed and rebuilt many times. It became a mental hospital in 1828. It was also used by Nazis as a prisoner of war camp during World War II.	BBC

This documents can also be used for Google Earth. You could use this document for a variety of topics like geography, history, wildlife, etc. Checkout Google for Educators. They have lots of wonderful ideas for classroom use.

Activity 27: Games in the classroom: How about having your students create their own game on topics of your choice. This lesson will give handouts to help your students be organized prior to the creation of their own game using a template from Microsoft PowerPoint.

Plan for the Game: The template titled **Game Plan** can be picked up in the **Game folder**. This document is intended to help your students stay organized and focused. You might want to get students in groups to make it more interesting. This plan can be customized for your classroom needs. If you plan on handing out this document because you don't have access to computers, hit the enter key in the last column of each row and hit the enter key to add more space for writing.

Game Plan

Directions: Come up with 16 questions or statements on any topic or theme. The teacher may specify what the topic will be about. Once you have come up with a question or statement, be sure to type in the answer under the answer column. You need every level of difficulty represented. Level 10 will obviously be a question that is easy to solve while level 160 will be the most difficult. The first one is done as an example for animals as the category. You can remove the example and use your own question depending on the theme or topic.

Tip: the question or statement has to give enough detail so that students can make a reasonable guess. The details in the question or statement can only apply to one possible answer. For example, if Cheetah was the answer, you wouldn't write "This large wild cat lives in Africa. It can catch its prey from its ability to travel at great speeds." This could easily apply to the Cheetah or Lion. You would need to additionally state that this animal has been clocked as fast as 70 miles per hour. This would be a level 10 because most middle school and high school students know this fact.

Question or Statement	Answer	Level
Name the endangered bird that is unique to North America. It is the national symbol of the United States.	Bald Eagle	10
		20
		30
		40
		50

Plan for the Game: The following is an example of what the plan might look like when students have completed their own plan for this project. The ratings might be considered very subjective. If time is an issue, different levels can be assigned to groups or individuals.

Question or Statement	Answer	Level
Name the threatened bird that is unique to North America. It is the national symbol of the United States. One of the largest nests on record of this bird weighed more than two tons.	Bald Eagle	10
What mammal is considered the most dangerous to humans, especially in urban areas when it comes to the transmission of diseases? In the late 1800s, doctors in China noticed that this mammal showed similar plague symptoms to people.	Rats	20
What mammal has been wiped out in parts of the world because farmers kill them to prevent them from eating their livestock? The average pack size of this mammal ranges from 8-9.	Wolf	30
This reptile is the heaviest lizard on earth. The saliva from this reptile has over 50 strains of bacteria. If its prey is struck by this creature, it will usually die within 24 hours.	Komodo Dragon	40
Name the snake that can reach 18 feet in length. It is the longest venomous snake in the world. They mostly live in the rain forests and plains of India and southern China.	King Cobra	50
If a predator snags this fish before it inflates, they will experience a foul taste and risk death. There are enough toxins in one of these fish that can kill 30 adult humans and there is no antidote.	Pufferfish	60
This bird was once endangered in the United States. Their population has made a comeback because of bans on the use of DDT and similar pesticides. They can dive at a speed of 200 miles an hour.	Peregrine Falcons	70

Peer Feedback

Directions: Look at another student's documentation and critique their work. Let them know where they have made mistakes. The first one has been done as an example.

Student Being Evaluated:	
Level	**Feedback**
10	When you represented the cheetah for level 10, you should have given more details about the speed it could reach. All the information you provided on the Cheetah could easily be considered information about lions as well.

Editing Based on Feedback

Directions: Get feedback from your peers. Determine if changes are necessary. If they aren't necessary, you need to state that in the proper column below. Be sure to update your changes in your **Final Plan**. The first one has been done as an example.

Level	Feedback from Peers	Changes you made. If not, why?
30	You mentioned that your mammal lives in Africa and that it lives in packs. You also stated that your animal is killed by farmers because they eat livestock. Additionally, you mentioned that your animal can take down wildebeest or antelope. All this information can easily apply to the African Wild Dogs. You could have added the additional fact that the animal being discussed can live as long as 25 years in the wild, since the African Wild Dog's life span is roughly 11 years in the wild.	The feedback from my peers was very helpful. I added the additional information that the animal can live up to 25 years in the wild.

Final Plan

Directions: Once you have received feedback from your peers, you can add your refined information to the proper leveled sections of the table below. The first level has been done as an example. You can replace the text in level 10 with your information.

Level	Level 10	Level 20	Level 30	Level 40
Statement/ Question	Name the threatened bird that is unique to North America. It is the national symbol of the United States. One of the largest nests on record of this bird weighed more than two tons.			
Answer	Bald Eagle			
Level	Level 50	Level 60	Level 70	Level 80
Statement/ Question				
Answer				
Level	Level 90	Level 100	Level 110	Level 120
Statement/ Question				
Answer				

Games: You can locate **Game** in the **Game folder.** This is the Game that reflects this entire lesson. This can be shown as an example so students can see what the final game will look like. Students can pick up the **GameTemplate** for editing. The template is very user friendly. Be sure to keep the original game template safe so students don't destroy the original.

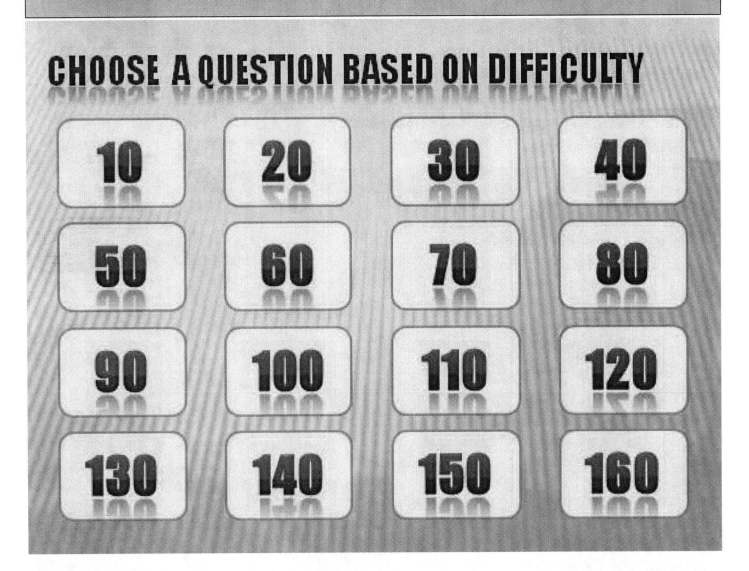

Game Tips: You can get game templates online for PowerPoint. Jeopardy templates are available online for free. This game was customized for this book. The following search will get you thousands of options: "jeopardy templates" + PowerPoint. You can also search PowerPoint + "game templates" to get other options. Once your students get the idea how to create games in PowerPoint, they can customize their own games.

Game Tip: To keep the game fair, put team names in a hat. All teams will go in order. If a team can't answer a question, pull a team's name from the hat. For example, if team one can't answer a question, a team will be drawn from the hat. If team one is drawn from the hat, then they can go again, otherwise, another team will have a chance to answer the question. Remove the team that was pulled from the hat until everyone has been equally represented. Once all their names have been drawn from a hat, all the names go back into the hat and the process starts over. Continue to ask questions in order and pulling teams from the hat if teams are unable to answer the question. You can always come up with your own rules. If you had buzzers, like in jeopardy, that would work too.

Keeping Score

Directions: Check off the proper rows for the team that earns the points

Points	Team 1	Team 2	Team 3	Team 4	Team 5	Team 6
10						
20						
30						
40						
50						
60						
70						
80						
90						
100						
110						
120						
130						
140						
150						
160						

Names in a Hat: The names in a hat was my student's idea. Until then, they were bickering about how to play the game. I learned my lesson the hard way!

Making Games in PowerPoint 2007: **Making Games in PowerPoint** can be picked up in the **Game folder.** This lesson will teach you and your students how to make a game in PowerPoint 2007 from scratch.

Directions: The following steps will assist you in creating games using Microsoft PowerPoint 2007. You can use the general concepts for 2003.

1. Open Microsoft PowerPoint by going to **Start | All Programs | Microsoft Office | Microsoft Office PowerPoint.**

2. The following window will pop up.

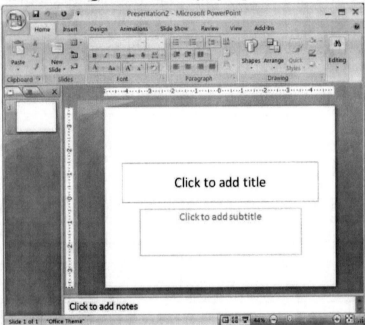

3. It would be a good habit to save the presentation. To save the presentation, click on the **Office** button. Choose the option and choose how you want to save the presentation.

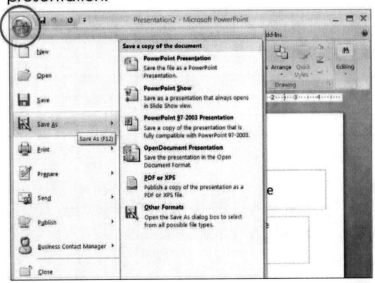

In this example, the presentation was saved for 97-2003 so that it can be presented on computers that don't have Office 2007.

CPSIA information can be obtained at www.ICGtesting.com
Printed in the USA
BVOW06s1503191014

371295BV00004B/33/P